Pauline Collins lives in London with her husband, fellow actor John Alderton, and their three children. She has been an actress for thirty years, appearing in such notable successes as *Upstairs Downstairs*, *No Honestly* and *Forever Green*. She created the title role in *Shirley Valentine* on stage and on screen, for which she received both the Tony and Olivier Awards, was nominated for an Oscar and won the British Academy Award.

Letter to Louise

Pauline Collins

CORGI BOOKS

LETTER TO LOUISE
A CORGI BOOK 0 552 13741 3

Originally published in Great Britain by Bantam Press,
a division of Transworld Publishers Ltd

PRINTING HISTORY
Bantam Press edition published 1992
Corgi edition published 1993

Set in 11/12½pt Linotype Plantin by
County Typesetters, Margate, Kent

Corgi Books are published by Transworld Publishers Ltd,
61–63 Uxbridge Road, Ealing, London W5 5SA,
in Australia by Transworld Publishers (Australia) Pty Ltd,
15–25 Helles Avenue, Moorebank, NSW 2170,
and in New Zealand by Transworld Publishers (NZ) Ltd,
3 William Pickering Drive, Albany, Auckland.

Reproduced, printed and bound in Great Britain by
Cox & Wyman Ltd, Reading, Berks.

For Lou, of course.
And also for two mothers,
hers, Maria, and mine, Nora.

Acknowledgements

Love and thanks to all the following:

My husband, John, without whose encouragement and continual support I would never have found the courage to write this book; my agent, Cat Ledger, fondly nicknamed 'The Gauleiter', who whipped a life-long procrastinator into action; Georgina Morley, an editor of remarkable patience and surprisingly little blue pencil; everyone at Transworld for putting their faith in a wholly untried writer; Janet Macklam, who translated my curiously shaped capitals into a readable manuscript; and finally special thanks to those who gave me permission to reveal their lives, Tony, Lou and Maria.

End

I remember the last time I saw you. We were about six feet apart.

The kind man held you on his left arm near a second door to the room I had not noticed before. 'Say goodbye to baby now.'

I made some dreadful kind of sob sound and you turned your head sharply and looked at me with a thousand-year-old stare and I knew this moment would be imprinted for ever in our memories; I in a navy suit of an ungiving material, you in white wool, with leggings hanging loose and too big where I had taken out the ribbons, because they seemed too tight.

And then the man and you slipped softly out of the room.

Every day of my life I've relived that moment, replayed each second like a book of flicker pictures, clinging frame by frame to the last images of you; your sharp-turned head and startled starfish hands slowly turning away, away, away from me as you disappeared through the door.

Through the years I planned this letter, this book. I wanted you to know; to have knowledge. Reading about adopted people, having one who is a close friend, the one thing they all want is information about themselves and their blood parents.

I began it many times, always with the intention that I would arrange for it to be given to your mother, and that she would make the ultimate choice of when, if ever, you should read it.

Most of all I wanted to answer the question that would be uppermost in your mind. Why did I do it? Why did I give you away?

Now in 1992, I still feel a blow in the solar plexus when I consider that question. I feel as if my soul is punched out through my throat.

Now in 1992, I cannot imagine why I did that terrible thing, why I didn't look harder for another solution.

Now in 1992, I am a little less arrogant in my self-sufficiency, a little more able to admit when I need help.

Now in 1992, I might have realized that you, Louise, are your own person and could rise above the difficulties of being an illegitimate daughter.

But in the summer of 1964, I couldn't see so clearly. I couldn't see hope – only despair – and so I made my choice.

Here now is something for you, a chronicle that may leave you a little wiser of how you came to be.

Killarney

I've always loved change: new beginnings. Even now I am more thrilled by a year that begins with the calendar a complete blank, than by the prospect of carefully orchestrated segues from job to job. Too much security makes me nervous; afraid of missing all the surprises just below the horizon.

One of the terrors of a little success is the possibility of losing the ability to dare, to jump off the cliff. Too many secure Mondays might make a person complacent. I've always loved Mondays and never understood 'that Monday morning feeling'. My Monday morning feeling is exhilaration, anticipation after the silence of the weekend.

Just one such Monday brought me to Killarney.

I'd answered an ad in *The Stage*:

KILLARNEY REPERTORY SEASON
New Irish Players require Assistant Stage-Managers. Male and Female. Play as Cast. London auditions.

It really appealed to me, that job. Not just rep but rep in another country, and that the birthplace of my grand-parents. Also I'd never been to Ireland.

Glendalough 1936

Five young Liverpool teachers tumbled shrieking, laughing, down the hill from St Kevin's Bed.

'*Don't forget now,*' *shouted the guide.* '*As you leave St Kevin's Bed, you'll meet the man you're going to marry.*'

At the bottom of the hill the girls banged into a group of fellows.

'*Oh God,*' *said Eileen.* '*Which one's mine?*'

'*Hello, Schubert.*' *The dark handsome one smiled at Nora Callanan, nicknamed for the bow she always wore in the back of her hair.*

'*How do you know my name?*' *said she, amazed.*

'*It's me! Tony McArdle. I'm Josie's brother.*'

'*Oh yes! How are you?*'

'*Fine. This is Jackie and Gus.*'

'*And who's that over there standing a little higher than anybody else?*'

'*That's Fat Collins. He's a London teacher.*'

'*Oh, you don't mix with the plebeians then?*'

'*A scholar forsooth,*' *smiled the young man on the hillock.*

'*Fat Collins meet Nora Callanan.*'

Three years later they were married. My parents.

I never knew how many takers Jim Mooney had, but having filled at least a page with my untried talents, I was auditioned in a small, London rehearsal room and a week or so later, learned I'd got the job.

Jim and I both recalled afterwards, that as I left I said: 'I hope you have me.'

'Oh, so do I,' said he, all red hair and energy and humour. Oh, the innocence of it.

I felt elated as the train pulled into Killarney Station. I hitched the window strap down and let the sweet, new air fill my lungs. That's my kind of litmus test for new places. Some delight. Some don't. No good reason. Just a kind of olfactory OK! New York and Calcutta are wonderfully similar, spicy, energized; Surrey is damp and draining; Wiltshire witchy, disturbing.

From the moment I smelled Killarney, I loved it. There was a sweetness and a blessing in the air that instantly befriends the soul. I've since felt that all over Ireland, but this was my very first taste.

I humped my suitcases down on to the platform; matching white Revelation, two sizes bought in recognition of my leaving home. I felt good, a little blasé even.

I felt quite smart too. I was wearing a butcher-boy hat, the height of fashion. It was a vaguely Dickensian affair, shaped like a soft almond tart, with a button in the middle and a jaunty peak over the brow. Mine was white straw and I loved it.

As I walked along the platform, empty of all but a handful of people, I saw a girl ahead of me, standing and looking towards me, also wearing a butcher-boy hat. Hers was brown velvet and sat cheekily on her strawberry curls. All at once mine began to feel a bit tacky and curiously tall on my beehive hair.

I knew, however, that the chic one was almost certainly a fellow actress.

'Are you for the theatre too?'

'Yes,' I said. 'Pauline, ASM, and small parts.'

'Jacqui, juvenile lead' . . . and she had a vanity case.

We decided to get a taxi together but a porter moved in with a barrow and a soft Kerry voice: 'Are 'oo for the Town Hall Theatre? I'll walk ye there.'

It must have been the hats.

Killarney was a station that impinged as little as possible on the scenery, a platform, a bit of a ticket office, then straight out past the Great Southern Hotel and into the town.

We followed our luggage past the jarveys waiting to give you a ride on the jaunting cars, past the tea and gift shop, along the grey walls of the demesne, with all the rhododendrons just beginning to bud.

It was all much smaller than I had expected, more compact, more like a little French town than anything in England; low-built pastelly buildings, shops with the name of the owner written large in a variety of scripts.

13

You couldn't always be sure what a shop sold, or whether indeed it mightn't be a bar. All the fronts were similar, some obscured by opaque glass.

And there was the Town Hall, a fairly decent pillared affair.

The porter took us in to a kind of marbled entrance hall, and unloaded our stuff.

'There ye are now. They'll all be across in the hall.' He gestured vaguely across a kind of grassy courtyard and left with his tip.

We looked around the entrance hall and saw the box-office and beneath it a sandwich-board displaying all our pictures.

Now Booking. New Irish Players
in a season of plays, direct from
the Abbey Theatre, Dublin.

(Carefully worded! Plays from the Abbey – not players.)

First Night. 28 May.

Dear God, less than three weeks away!

Jacqui and I walked across the grassy yard until we came to an open door. We looked in, and saw a hall filled with stacking chairs like those found in a school, and on our right a good big stage. We heard voices and banging, and couldn't see anyone.

'Let's have a look in there.' She pointed to a door half open, on the other side. That led us into a bit of corridor at the end of which lay two big rooms. In the second, I saw Jim, banging a mirror into place. The room was filled with trunks and clothes-rails, and sitting in the midst of chaos with a cup of coffee, was a tiny, round, good fairy with a beautiful face. Jim looked up as we came in.

'You're here. You made it. Great!'

The lady came over, smiling, to shake hands. 'Welcome to Killarney. I hope you'll be very happy with us.'

'This is Pat,' said Jim. 'Pat Turner, Co-producer. Leading character lady.'

'Come and sit down and have a cup of tea. Then you can go off and find your digs . . .'

Now I'd pictured all kinds of first footings in Killarney, many of them centring round lovely pubs and Guinness and soda-bread teas, but having to find myself somewhere to live had never occurred to me. Jacqui, however, was a seasoned tourer. She asked for the Accommodation List, which looked massive, but it seemed most of the company had got there before us, and had bagged not only the best, but also all known addresses where they 'kept people'.

However, with assurances that all we had to do was bang on a few doors, and we'd be OK, away we went, Jacqui and I, up and down the streets of Killarney. A soft rain had started.

I am naturally a rather shy person, so to take the curse off this humiliating experience I found myself affecting a plaintive Irish accent after the fifth door or so.

'Do ye keep people?'

Those we disturbed were kindness itself with one brusque exception – 'No theatricals.' Bang.

We were given tea, scones, potato cakes, advice, opinions, further addresses, but no beds.

As the day wore on the rain set in softly but persistently. Jacqui's corduroy-velvet hat remained relentlessly chic and her curls unbowed. Mine lost its crispness within the first half-hour and by six o'clock looked like a failed meringue. We were sodden and hopeless by the time we returned to the theatre.

There we met another company member, Joan Steynes.

'Ah, God, look at them. Come on down to our digs and let's see if there's a corner for you.'

71 New Street was the best digs in town – run by two sisters – Sally and Cis – they didn't just keep people. It was their vocation. Not just lodgings, proper digs, very near the theatre – four meals a day. Lodgers' sitting-room. £3.10s per week.

'I have a room,' said Sal, 'but it's reserved for a teacher. However, you can have it till she takes up the post. You'll have to share a double bed.'

Jacqui was not delighted at this prospect. I would happily have slept with three sailors and a dog.

It was a wonderful room – an attic, stretching right across the top floor, with two huge windows overlooking New Street. It was well furnished but, because the floor was roughly polished boards, it had an air of almost monastic simplicity. There was a low chair by the window, a plain rug in the middle of the room.

We went downstairs and met Cis, the older and quieter of the two sisters. They were a perfect team, Sal and Cis. Sally was the 'front man', Junoesque, always frocked and heeled, with a ready smile. But there was a firm glint in the eyes behind her specs, that ensured there was an order of things. Meals were served and eaten on time. The sitting-room was available but not taken for granted. The house was ours but not all of it. There was an unspoken understanding that discouraged the lodgers from straying into Sal's quarters or the back kitchen.

That was Cis's domain, Cis with her gentle smile and her poor feet spreading out of her slippers. I never saw her seated. Ever. Whenever I snuck in to say hello, she would be propped against the range on one tired leg, yellow-white hair drifting round her exhausted parchment face. I know she slept because I once glimpsed a nether region beyond the back kitchen. A bit of a bed, a cupboard, swiftly closed behind a door.

But that first evening I'd only seen the main kitchen when we sat down to our inaugural meal at New Street.

Joan was already seated with two other members of the

company when we came down. John McMahon, who must have been in his mid-sixties then, stately, striking, glamorous in the way of McLiammoir and McMaster. He shrugged off his greatcoat with the shoulder cape, as Sally leaned over him with the oxtail soup.

He eyed us, the new girls, as he lifted off his broad-brimmed hat and put it on the window ledge.

'So now you're the new blood.' He had a fairly strong north of Ireland accent, coming as he did from just outside the six counties, and this gave him a rather dismissive manner. I got the impression as we talked that he had little time for young ones of either sex. But he did look incredibly like my grandfather Callanan, and beneath the gold-rimmed glasses I thought I saw great humour. I wasn't wrong.

Tucked in the corner watching us while we had the once-over from John, was a thin and whimsical elf. 'Hello, I'm Liam. Liam Sweeney.' Little smiling mouth, rabbity teeth. 'You're very welcome.'

He sat smoking instead of soup, legs crossed and arms laced over his thigh with his ciggie dangling loosely in his right hand between drags.

As Sally was bringing in steaming plates of stewed lamb with dumplings, the door burst open and in came a rosy-faced woman with snowy hair.

'Kitty, you're late.'

'Sally, I'm up to my eyes in hem-lines.' Kitty slumped into her chair. Then sat bolt upright, spreading her fingers on the table. 'Look at my hands. The veins are bursting out of them. If I see another full skirt, I'll scream. And I've no eyes left at all.'

Kitty. Kathleen O'Sullivan, alteration hand at Hilliards Department Store. She was probably sixty then. Cosy, funny and very open to anything that life brought her way. She was not married and between her and John McMahon there crackled a familiar *badinage*. I think she once made a pass at him and he'd fled in terror. She was one of the most loving people I'd met in my life and as far as I know she never found anyone to give it to.

After dinner we walked up the road into Main Street with Liam and Joan. Liam was wearing jeans. They didn't really suit his little thin legs, but they were real Levi's bought in Canada where he'd done some work. They took us for a drink in the Grand Hotel next to the theatre. I drank schooners of sherry the size of teacups, and felt as though my real life was beginning. I was not yet twenty-three and away from home for the first time.

That night as I lay in bed with Jacqui, wishing I was on the window side nearer the sky and the lights, she turned to me and said, 'If I roll into you in the night, it's not because I fancy you.'

February 1942

I love it here.

Everything is bright and whitey. There's a white pillar behind Mama and me. And a white tablecloth. A man is bending over me with a dish. I like him, because he's smart and has a black bow on his shirt and smooth black hair.

'Here we are, little maid.'

I'm excited and can't stop breathing fast. Mama helps me with my spoon but I can do it. I can do it! I'm a grown-up girl.

'What a grown-up girl. How old is she?'

'Eighteen months.'

'My, my, my. What a clever girl. Anything else, madam?'

'Just a pot of tea.'

I love this place.

December 1942

Mag lets me play with the dollies again today, china dollies.

She sits me on the soft couch in the front-room and opens the cabinet and takes out all the china dollies and lays them beside me on the big cushion. I like the little boy and girl best. They're very, very small. I lay them on the cushion and cover them with a lace doily. They're my babies.

Maggie May is in and out.

'I won't break them, Mag.'

'I know you won't, my sweetheart. You're my grown-up girl.'

I love Mag.

We live in Mag's house. We live in the big front bedroom. Mama and Dada in the big bed, me on a camp bed and Gabe in the cot.

I love our room at night because the street lights make patterns on the walls and I can hear the people walking and laughing.

Jack lives here too – up more stairs. Mama says he's another lodger. What's a lodger? He's handsome and I love him. I'm his best girl.

In the little room on the half-landing is Julie, Mag's auntie. In the day she sits in the big chair in the kitchen. She's round and old.

February 1943

Denzil and Graham gave me a pig. I think it's a pig. It might be a beetle. I thought they said pig. Maybe pig-beetle. I love it. It's my friend. It's black and shiny with two wiggling shaped ears. And it runs quite fast. I gave it a flower to eat; a yellow primrose. I think it's full now.

It wasn't a pig. I've seen a pig now and it's very big and dirty. It was a beetle but it ran into the heather and I can't find it. Maybe I'll have a pig now.

The next morning Jacqui and I walked up New Street

to the Parish Hall where rehearsals would be held.

Joan walked with us, incredibly smartly dressed in a well-cut beige skirt, crimson jumper and matching shoes, very high heels. She had a great figure, was witty, attractive, about thirty-five then, but not married. Were the men of Dublin mad? She was a trained nurse and when not touring she lived with her mother in Dublin. There was a man – but not for marrying.

It was sharp and bright in the May morning and I felt that uplifting, breathcatching exhilaration you get when the season changes.

We found our way through a garden, round the back of the hall, and up some dusty stairs to a huge room with five big windows.

Round a long refectory table most of the company was already seated. This is the moment that we in the theatre in time grow accustomed to. More than most jobs, I suppose our profession is like one encounter group after the other.

This is the moment in each job when you meet the people who are about to become closer than family over the next few months. These are the people you will trust nightly with your talent, your vulnerability, your strength. They are the people to whom you will be forced to turn for companionship and support. You wouldn't necessarily choose them, but you will grow to understand them and therefore to love them – an arranged marriage.

There was always, too, the possibility of romance! Today might be the day I found the love of my life.

A quick shufti at the company round the table in the Parish Hall that morning told me that there was no immediate threat to my virginity. There were two late-middle-aged character actors, Noel Dalton and Cecil Sheehan.

Noel had rheumy eyes and a terrible wheeze which was not helped by his chain-smoking. He had a yellow stain which seemed to run from his fingers, up his arm, over his teeth, through his moustache and up to his hair. He was very gentle and easy-going.

Cecil by contrast was a sharp-witted Cork man – a baker in Dublin in the winter.

Jacqui's opposite, the male juvenile, was a nice but intense young man called Stephen whose very pretty wife was on his arm and at his side for the duration.

Pat and Jim presided over us all with a warmth and affection that made me feel uniquely at home. I'd never been a member of a company before for any length of time and I liked the sensation that we had a long way to go together.

Yet to come was the male ASM, Vincent Smith, on his way from Dublin. Maybe my dream man?

So there we all sat listening to Jim explaining his way of working: rehearse three plays in the three-week rehearsal period. Working plan: Saturday opening with a repertoire of three, then continue to rehearse as we played until we had ten plays.

We offered a different show every night, so each morning there was a ten o'clock call to fit up and dress the new set – except on Sundays when the call was after ten o'clock Mass. Sundays? We played Sundays? Gasps of disbelief from the English contingent. Nobody ever plays Sundays. Yes they do. I also sensed a certain terror in those who did not dig with the left that they were to be dragged into some papist net, trapped into religious observations that they did not hold with.

'Mass, I take it, is not obligatory,' said Jacqui firmly. Jaze no!

I was astonished as we read the first play, *The Country Boy* by John Murphy. Amazed at the beauty of it, the humour and the sadness of it. I think I was expecting a farce or a mystery, run-of-the-mill weekly rep stuff. Not here! Still in my opinion one of the best plays I've ever performed.

I was surprised too that when Jim read out our

21

characters, I had a really good part: Eileen, a young girl in love with Curly, the juve lead.

I could see Jacqui was a bit fed up about this. She had a wonderful character. The leading lady, forty-year-old alcoholic wife of the returned Yank. But she was only twenty-seven, and was very put out to be playing an older woman.

Still everybody settled into work and as the week went by I began to feel more and more that I had come home. You know that feeling when all your energies are flowing in the right direction, you're going with the current and all seems right with the world.

I was relieved when Jim decided that my duties as ASM were to dress the set and sit on the book as prompter for the other plays in which my parts would be very small. I was spared the humiliation of everyone finding out that my 'cleating' was below standard. Cleating is the action of joining two flats together with ropes by means of deftly lassoing two adjoining hooks of metal with one casual upward flick of the wrist. I've never got the hang of it.

By about Thursday of the first week's rehearsals, a kind of unease was to be felt in the Parish Hall. Stephen, playing the part of Curly, the brother who stayed at home, and Jim playing the *emigré* and directing, were finding that they had very different ideas about acting. Stephen had been Stanislavski-trained, after a fashion, and wouldn't learn his lines or say one until it felt right. With three plays to rehearse before opening, Jim was understandably driven yampy.

By Friday Stephen and Jim had amicably agreed that he should be 'let go'.

By Saturday Jacqui decided that the delights of Killarney and forty-year-old leading ladies were not for her. She was out of the town by midday. One night too many sharing a double bed with me no doubt.

Jim and Pat then spent the weekend routing through

22

the CVs of those he'd auditioned in London, looking for replacements. Meanwhile, the part of Curly went to Liam. We were delighted to be playing opposite each other.

We heard each other's lines till we were cross-eyed and by Sunday-night dinner, Kitty decided the best thing for everyone was to go to the dance.

Now every Sunday, there was a dance somewhere. In some hotel or hall there would be one of the big showbands or one of the lesser ones belting out dance music, always with a singer, miked to carry fifty miles round the countryside.

It was an entertainment, an introduction bureau, a licensed grope, an opportunity for great conviviality and a possibility for great loneliness.

We went as a gang, Joan, Kitty and her younger friend Mary, me, and Liam, squiring us all. This one was at the Gleneagles Hotel in a great barn of a hall with the boys one end and the girls the other. Seated on benches between were the ever-hopeful pushing forty or fifties, still on the lookout for that farmer's son living with his mother, who might be persuaded to change one safe haven for another.

I don't know why it was then that so many men wouldn't leave their mothers. Maybe it was that those who did, left utterly, for England or America, and for a different kind of woman from Brooklyn or Liverpool or Manchester.

Liam got us all started with a dance apiece, and then we were on the market. I was whirled around, stamped on, breathed on and groped by a variety of beaux until I finally settled for a quiet boy with red hands from out the country. I've always hated dancing, I have no messages from head to legs, but no one ever believes me. Declan and I sorted out a kind of gentle motoring movement that took nothing out of us. He was a good-natured soul who stood me several sherries and a vodka. I liked him apart from his rather strange smell. I found out later he worked at a slaughterhouse.

I go to Miss Lacy's school.

You just go past the goats behind our house and there's the school. It's not really our house. It's Miss Lacy's. But she's got a bigger one.

I wish I could go all day to school. I only go in the morning. If you go all day you can have a hot potato off the stove. Once I took one. It was Venetia's and her Dada gives Miss Lacy coal, so she shouted at me. I had to stand behind the dressing-up curtain in disgrace. It was quite a long time so I put some of the clothes on and peeped out with different hats. To make them laugh. Miss Lacy didn't.

Anyway Mama makes me potato cakes and lovely food and I have milk in a little jug from the goats.

'Close your eyes.'

Dada's just come in from camp and he's looking smiling and secret. It's quite dark and I'm sitting on the edge of the hearth in my nightie.

I put my hands over my eyes. I feel like a picture in a book. I feel quite pretty, because my nightie has flowers on it. Also good. Mama let me stay up because I'm a good girl. I played with Gabe. I made her laugh. I put lots of hats on and made them fall off and said, 'Whoops.' And every time I said 'Whoops' in a special way, Gabe laughed so much she fell over.

'Now keep your eyes closed — tight! And hold out your arms.'

Something soft and silky is jumbling in my arms and snuffling and licking.

'Can I open them now?' I do.

It's a puppy! Blacky, browny, wriggly.

'Oh, Dada.' I'm hugging Dada's legs and the puppy and Mama's smiling and holding Gabe.

I love the puppy.

I love my Dada. He's a sergeant.

I love my Mama and my Gabe.

Christmas 1943

I've swallowed a baby penny. The one with a robin on the back. Every time I go to the lav I listen for the clink. Mama says it'll come through eventually.

I've stopped going on the chamber now. I go out the back. It's quite cold and a bit tall, but I feel grown up. It's like a big round oil drum with a seat and a lid. In Maggie May's we had a proper lav and you pulled the chain.

Every night we put threepence on the lid and Mr Dodds comes to empty it. Frank calls him Fairy Nightshit.

Everyone's here for Christmas. Grandad, Frank and Auntie. Maurice couldn't make it. He's in Gib. It was funny yesterday, Mama showed me a photo of when they were all little. It was all browny coloured and they were all looking serious. Mama and Auntie were holding hands, with long knickers and bows in their hair. And Maurice was in the front leaning against Uncle Phil because Uncle Phil's the big brother. And Frank! Frankie was only a baby and now he's a grown-up sailor. Frank's in his uniform now. I wish Uncle Phil and Auntie Nora would bring little Phil and Marg for Christmas but it's too far.

Mama's fitting everyone in. There's two camp beds but one of them sags when you put it together. Frank's going to sleep between two chairs. I want to do that. Grandad's having my little bed. Maybe I'll go in with Mama and Auntie.

By Monday morning we were all agog to know how the rehearsals would go with the new Curly and a diminished company.

Liam was great. His natural wistfulness and gentle persona were perfect for the brother who hadn't dared leave home. By midday we had a new leading lady.

I couldn't believe it when Maggie Hickey turned up in Killarney. We'd been at the 'Sacred Heart', Hammersmith, together. We hadn't known each other well. Her sister Bridget was my age; Maggie a year or two younger. The red hair and creamy skin left us in little doubt that this was another child of Irish grandparents. She arrived among us, shining, dark-brown eyes glowing with delight. Imagine the feeling when you've lost a job and then against all odds it's yours again!

Because of the recasting traumas, Jim decided that opening with three plays was now a bit ambitious and we would rehearse just one other: *Is The Priest At Home?*, a comedy centred round a parish priest and his relations with his parishioners; much of the plot hinged on the embattled stance of two elderly men, one an Orangeman, the other a Catholic. John McMahon, cross-eyed with rage and narrow vowels, and Cecil Sheehan, villainous and twinkling with his lovely Cork accent. I had a good part in this too. A schoolteacher with a romance on much of the time – no stage-managing again. Hallelujah.

On Tuesday we all went to the theatre to have a stagger through on the stage.

I was early, to make the tea, and as I walked across the courtyard, lying asleep in the sun, his head on his case, was a golden-haired, ruddy-faced Adonis with forearms like a longshoreman. This must be the other ASM.

I woke him up with a mug of tea.

'Jasus fuckin' Christ, wha' time is it?'

'Half-past nine.'

'Jaze, who the fuck are you?'

I filled him in a bit on the story so far, and fell instantly in love with this saviour who was to be the true stage-manager, cleater extraordinaire.

I would have stayed in love with Vincent Smith for ever had it not been for the fact that he would never utter a word to you without a 'Come 'ere till I tell you' and a dig in the ribs or arm.

After a week of giggles and jabs, I still loved him but the ardour diminished as the bruises increased.

He'd come up from Dublin on the four o'clock mineral water lorry, so was understandably knackered. There was a five o'clock Electricity Supply Board (E.S.B.) lorry but that would have been cutting it a bit fine. Many people in those days used the big delivery firms as an economical form of transport. The trips were regular so it was like a kind of underground timetable. Reliable, the drivers were generous-spirited. You could maybe buy them a meal if you could afford it or a drink, but they really did it out of goodness.

Vincent demonstrated instantly that he knew exactly what was required. He had the prompt corner and the sound system organized within a couple of hours, and then set about making a prompt copy of our first two plays.

The next day, Wednesday, 21 June, about lunch-time, I looked out of the window of the Parish Hall and saw a pale-faced man with black curly hair, marching below me, frowning, looking for a way in. Maggie and I waved out of the window.

'Do you want us? Are you the new man?'

He continued to frown, disconcerted, caught out in some way.

'I want the New Irish Players. I'm Tony Rohr. I'm late.'

'Yes,' said we. 'Come on in.'

'Is that the new man?' said Jim, breaking off the rehearsal. 'Great.'

Tony leapt up the stairs of the Parish Hall and found

himself in that disconcerting situation of being lastcomer to a group. All eyes on the newcomer – can he act? Is he good company? Will he buy a drink?

Somebody gave him a cup of tea and then we went back to rehearsing *The Country Boy*.

We were doing a scene towards the end of the play when the truth is out – America's streets are not paved with gold – they're strewn with the lost dreams of the incomers, all wishing they'd stayed at home. Everyone was terrific in the scene, true and moving. Maggie and Jim as the Yanks, Pat and John, the old parents, and Liam and I as the impressionable young, their illusions shattered. Towards the end I had a song to sing, 'The Last Rose of Summer'. It was the first time I'd tried it in playing.

'There won't be a dry eye in the house,' said John when I'd finished.

We could see that Tony was surprised at what we'd achieved, and found the company maybe a bit more ambitious than he'd expected – as I had.

Flushed with that good feeling when work's going well, Jim called an early lunch and we all piled into O'Leary's bar next door.

'Will you all have a jar?' said Tony. Aah. 'It's my birthday.'

In the course of the jar, we learned that his mother was from Tipperary although she now lived in London with Tony's stepfather, as he did himself. Playing Sundays held no terror for him. Nor did ten o'clock Mass. He was very different now from when we first saw him with his serious, puzzled face. Gone, the slightly hunted, severe look; when he smiled, his face betrayed all kinds of wit and wickedness. Watching his easy charm and humour I thought, How could Jim have chosen the other chap in the first place? Looking round at the group now, at Maggie and Tony slotting comfortably into place, I thought, This is a family – all these people belong

28

together. I realized too that not one of us was not; to some degree, a Celt.

Everyone went back to rehearsal, energized by good work and good company.

Tony went off round the town to find digs, and to read Number Three play in which he had a 'small but telling' part of 'The Boots'. *He* had a song in that. There's nothing like a bit of a song you know for grabbing the audience and leaving them with a memory of you.

After rehearsals Maggie and I went to have our hair done at a salon where the company had 'an arrangement' – a trial run. Cheap hair-dos in exchange for a credit in the programme. We arrived in this very large, slightly old-fashioned salon, filled with the cream of Killarney society and a hotbed of gossip and support.

We both had long hair which we fondly imagined would be kept shining and glamorous by a twice-weekly trip to 'Queenie's'.

Queenie herself supervised the trimming and setting of our hair on rather small (I thought) rollers and personally stood by with a fully loaded firm-hold lacquer spray with which she fixed our back-combed tresses into immovable wodges of curls.

'There now! That'll last a treat. Doesn't it look great?'

'Lovely. Thank you very much.' Cowards that we were.

We scattered down the stairs, rolling our eyes in mute despair. 'Ooh God.'

We went to the Grand for a little drink, feeling that the hair had to be taken for a last libation before being shot at dawn. It was quite early yet and no one much about to witness the incongruity of full-dress hair worn with dusty rehearsal pants and jumpers. Across from us sat a pleasant-faced young man in a tightish brown suit. Lots of suits looked like that in the sixties, barely containing the chest, the bum, the thighs of those encased in them. It was as if those bodies knew the revolution was just

29

around the corner. Next year would bring the Beatles and Flower Power, loose clothes and free love—

'How are you, girls?' – but not yet.

'Great.'

'Would you like a sherry?'

'Well thanks, that'd be lovely.'

Eamonn worked for the German crane factory. A junior executive. Much had been promised by the Germans when they brought their industry to Killarney. Huge numbers of jobs, prosperity, expansion. For the locals, so far, not much was in evidence. After three years no local man held anything above a very junior post. Still there was a glamour attached to those who were on its payroll and Eamonn felt confident as he chatted up the birds.

'The hair looks great.'

'Thanks.' Yuk.

'Are you going out tonight?'

'No, we're learning lines.'

We were still naïve enough to enjoy the reaction that such revelations could be guaranteed to provoke.

'Oh, you're actresses. How do you remember all that stuff?'

We filled Eamonn in on the glamour and torment of theatrical life, the camaraderie, our girlish hopes and dreams. He in turn riveted us with the cut and thrust of life amongst the Euro-cranes. We were equals, young, up and coming, in our own spheres.

We offered him a short which he refused and then—

'You know, girls, I hope you don't mind me saying – it's a bit stiff.'

'What?'

'A bit high – the hair.'

'We know.'

'I have a friend with a lovely modern salon. Meet me here tomorrow, and I'll introduce you.'

'OK. See you tomorrow.'

'Bye.'

Home then to New Street. Dinner and lines, and gossip about the new man.

Spring 1944

I'm collecting sand for the porch of my doll's house.

A soldier helped me to put it in the envelope. He's got a different sign on his uniform. A maple leaf. He's from Canada.

Just along the lane someone is crying. I can see the Colonel's wife and her little girl. They've both got beautiful dresses with white collars. Pink dresses. The lady is hitting a poor dirty girl on the head.

'I told you to bring the milk, you're useless. Go on. Get off. Your brother can do it. Johnny, you do it.'

A dirty boy runs off with the milk can.

The poor crying girl is sitting by the side of the road.

'Never mind. Do you want to help me collect sand?'

The girl gets up. She's quite big, bigger than me. She's very dirty all over. Her hair is sticking up and short and her face is dusty and rosy with tear-marks on her cheeks. Her frock has bits hanging down from it and her shoes are nearly falling off. Her cardigan is all torn and has bits of food on it. She's like The Little Matchgirl. I think she's a ragamuffin. I love her.

'Oi 'ate 'er. Wanna see moi treasures?'

She takes my hand and we go along the lane and into a wood. I've never been this far before. Angie suddenly squats down by a tree and I can see her awful knickers.

''Ere they are.'

She puts her hand into the hole of the tree and brings out a newspaper parcel. She's unfolding the paper very carefully and shows me her treasures.

There's a little doll's bath and a black comb, a bit broken, and a holey kettle.

'Oi keep 'em 'ere else th'ole feller 'ave 'em off me.'

'I like that doll's bath.'

'Want it?'

'No, it's yours.'

She wraps everything up and hides it away again.

'Come 'n 'ave dinner.'

'All right.'

We're going further into the woods but soon it's lighter and there's the lane. Is it my lane? I can't see my house. Angie takes me by the hand into a small dark shed. It's a house! There's a thin lady cooking on a stove. There's one armchair with a man sitting in it. There are lots of children bigger than me and two babies. A big baby in a pram and a little baby in a cot. Everyone is raggedy. I think these are the raggle-taggle gypsies.

'This is my friend. She's three.'

'Give 'er a spoon,' says Angie's Mum.

We all stand round the table and the lady puts a big pot in the middle and we all dig in. It's lovely, it's like hotpot.

The little baby is very small and quiet and has quite a nice frock on, but the big one is shouting and has no trousers, just a jumper. I think it must be a bit cold in that pram. No covers at all. Also it's got a little thing sticking out of its front bottom. I don't know what that is.

'I'm cold now.'

'Give 'er yer jumper.'

'Angie put my arms in her grey cardigan. It's nice and warm but smells a bit of dinner.

'Where she live?'

'Down boi Lacy's.'

'Take 'er 'ome.'

'I'm too tired. I want to stay here.'

'You can't stay 'ere. What you Mam say? Put 'er in with the baby. Push 'er 'ome.'

So off we go. Me in the pram with the big baby and Angie and her big sister and Johnny. On the way the baby wees in the pram out of his little thing. I haven't got one like that. I think I'd better get out of the way of that.

When we come towards our house I can see Mama looking out.

'Where have you been?'

'With my friend.'

Mama has a special face – a worried face and another face like when she's cleaning out the tin bath. But she's smiling too.

'Thank you for minding her. But you mustn't ever go away again without telling me. Would you like some tea?'

Everyone would.

'It's a lovely afternoon. Let's have it on the grass.'

Mama makes a lovely tea with the blue check cloth and butterfly cakes and sandwiches and cups of tea. The baby loves the grass and does another wee-wee and then Mama finds a pair of knickers for him.

They're all going now and I feel very sad. I want them to stay. Mama has given Angie her jumper back and we wave goodbye.

I'm in the tin bath now. Mama boiled two pans and she's washing me a lot, with a bit of Dettol in the water.

'Can I go there again?'

'We'll see.' Her special washing face.

'I love Angie.'

'I know.'

'Are they ragamuffins?'

'Tinkers probably.'

I'm sad. 'I thought they were the raggle-taggle gypsies.'

After rehearsal the next day, Maggie and I went off to the salon to meet Eamonn and his friend, Dan, a handsome smart boy, similarly bursting out of a sensible brown suit. Into the backwash the two of us went. Goodbye firm hold. Goodbye curls.

Dan had the touch. You could tell as soon as he laid hands on your hair, you knew he was in charge – deft sweeps of the brush, directing the hair into a lush brown curtain, culminating in a casual yet determined flick. I wasn't used to wearing my hair down. Till now it had been a complicated affair, starting with a kind of chrysanthemum-shaped waterfall on top, achieved by dividing a chunk off in an elastic band and backcombing it over the rest, which was pinned up in a french pleat held together by huge numbers of clips.

Dan encouraged me to have a bit off the bottom and wear it loose for some of the parts I was to play. It was hell at first, doing without my top knot. I felt very short and flat-headed. But gradually I got used to a more natural look and even dared to have a fringe cut. Good old Dan.

We took the boys for a drink and so enjoyed their company that we arranged to have a night out with them at the Europa Hotel the next week. The Europa was a newly built, multi-storey, German hotel on the lake shore, the outside of which had nothing whatever to do with its environment. It was ultra modern, too high and bright yellow amidst the muted colours of the Kerry Hills. But in those days we didn't really hold much of a torch for beauty. We wanted a bit of excitement and sophistication.

Back at New Street at dinner-time, news had travelled before me.

'Now,' said John McMahon. 'You and that Hickey one have been seen in the Grand with two fellers.'

'So we were, John. Eamonn from the crane factory and Dan the hairdresser.'

'Oh, God. A hairdresser, Dan the man,' said he, crossing his eyes and tightening his vowels. 'You don't want to be messing about with those town boys. You get on with your work. You've a tough season ahead.'

'John! We had a drink with them, that's all and Dan's doing our hair for us.'

'Well, just so long as you don't get caught up in that flighty crowd!'

I suddenly had an uncontrollable desire to scream with

laughter. Here was I, my first job away from home, nearly twenty-three. Fancy-free and getting more discipline from John McMahon than I would from my own father.

'Ah, shut up, John,' said Joan. 'One port in the Grand is hardly an invitation to unbridled sexual promise.'

'And she paid,' said Kitty, winking at me over her apple pie. No secrets here then.

At the end of the week a gang of us decided to go to the pictures, to the Sunday matinée. We were all shell-shocked from learning the second play at night, while rehearsing *The Country Boy* by day. Our brains needed some undemanding entertainment to blank out the welter of words we'd been holding in our heads. That first week of role-learning made me the most tired I'd ever been. When not gadding with the unsuitable Dan and Eamonn, I would climb up to my lovely peaceful room at the top of the house and sag in a heap over the dancing words. It got easier as the season went on, the old brain got familiar with the weekly assault on its capabilities and came up trumps.

The cinema in Killarney was then in a kind of a field beyond the station, more of a barn than an Odeon, its interior an indeterminate wine colour, the seats unyielding and of questionable cleanliness. Down at the front were benches where the kids sat and fought their way cheerfully through every film, regardless of its content.

This particular Sunday there was a really good film advertised and a crowd was lined up outside the doors well ahead of opening time, to get good seats.

Two-thirty came and went and still the doors remained shut and no sign of life anywhere in the building. By three, rumbles of discontent began to permeate the waiting hordes.

'Paddy, where are you?'

'Get these bloody doors open.'

'Will we break 'em down?'

Around twenty past three there was movement round the side of the cinema and a hush fell over the crowd. From the little side door a small, sandy figure appeared – a boy of about eleven.

'There's no matinée today. Me daddy's gone . . .' the small voice tailed away, lost in the mutterings of the crowd.

'What do you say?'

'There's no matinée today, me daddy's gone to . . .'

'What?'

'Me daddy's gone to the races in Tralee.'

After this announcement, the unfortunate messenger very wisely legged it away into the safety of distance and the family homestead.

In all our time in Killarney, we never made it to a Sunday matinée. The races won every time.

Maggie and Tony and Joan and I went for a walk instead, in the demesne, damp and lush, and when it began to rain in earnest, we headed back to a little café we'd seen over the gift shop near the Intercontinental Hotel. We enjoyed Tony's company. We hadn't seen much of him that week because he wasn't in *The Country Boy*, and was on his own in digs in the new estate. I think he was a bit isolated. It's hard enough joining a company late, but then if you're not working either, you don't have the same uncomplicated socializing as everyone else. However, he'd found a friendly host in Con O'Leary in O'Leary's bar and we promised to give that a go instead of the Grand.

It was sheer indulgence for Joan and me to eat a late tea, knowing we'd dinner at six-thirty, but the lovely little sandwiches and scones with jam and cream were too hard to resist, and we were very taken with the waitress who ran the place. A sweet-faced, middle-aged lady with tired legs and a willing heart, Mrs B.

She was delighted to get to know us and went to all the plays every season. She liked to compare performances from year to year in the plays that came round again, like *The Country Boy* and *The Tender Trap*. She took a great shine to Tony and bet her bottom dollar he was Curly this year.

'Well you've just lost it, missus,' said he. 'But I know I'd be great in that part.'

'Aah so's Liam,' I said, loyal to my mate, but I kind of knew that he was right.

Mrs B piled vast quantities of scones on our table, many more than the regulation two per tea.

'We've made too many, help us out.'

We gathered our 1s 3d per tea and added 6d for a tip.

'So long, Mrs B, see you next week.'

I arranged to meet Tony and Maggie and Vincent after dinner that night, and we all went to the dance. It was the Desi Mulholland Showband at the Cahernane. We hung around on the road out, waiting for a lift; the four of us plus Liam and Kitty and Mary, a daunting group for most motorists. But eventually a big van stopped with three cheery brothers in the front.

'We'll give ye a lift if ye all dance with us.'

'What, me too?' said Vincent.

'Go 'way with ye – in ye get.'

Kitty could barely make it into the back of the van and one of the brothers got out to give her a leg up while Tony and Vincent hauled from above. She was such a sociable, joyous person, Kitty. I mean, can you imagine being over sixty, single, in a small town and still going out with a hopeful heart to the Sunday dance?

'Now, missus,' said the carroty one, 'that'll be the first dance.'

'You're on,' said Kitty.

That was a great night. It was a really good band who drew a big crowd too. There was none of that desolate echo you get with the more desultory groups.

The carrot brothers were fantastic dancers, energetic

exhibitionists, and to be avoided at all costs by floor-shunters like myself. Kitty and Mary had a brilliant evening and I loved watching Tony and Maggie experience it all for the first time. They danced well both together and with loads of other people. I drifted round a bit gently with Liam, when I saw a familiar face, smiling and giving a little wave with a red hand.

'Good night, how are you?'

'Declan!' I was really pleased to see him.

'Will we have a dance – or a drink and then a dance?'

'Let's have a quick dance and a long drink.'

Declan grinned. 'All right, so.'

I felt comfortable with him. We chuntered sedately round the periphery of the hall like old friends.

Afterwards at the bar I found that we talked easily about our lack of prowess on the dance floor.

'Why do you come so?'

'Well, I'm with my friends from the company, and I enjoy the band, and the atmosphere. Why do you?'

Declan studied his red hands intently. 'I suppose because I want to meet someone – someone to go for a walk with or for a picnic on the lake shore.'

'And is there no one near where you live – no one at work?'

'No, it's very quiet out there. Just the mammy and I.' Aah, the mammy. 'No close neighbours. So I have to make a bit of an effort.'

12.15 a.m. Liam shouts across the room that the redheads are giving us a lift back. God love them.

'Good night, Declan, see you again.'

'Next week maybe?'

'Maybe – maybe one day, if we all go out for a picnic, you could come with us?'

'That'd be great.'

A moment of embarrassment.

'Come on, Pauline.'

The red hand raised in salute.

'Good night, Declan.'
I like him.

Summer 1944

We're in a lovely new house. It's made of brick not wood, like Russets. It's Mrs Castle's but we're keeping it for a long while 'til we go home after the war. I wonder where home is? I thought it was Mag's.

Maybe it was Denton Drive where I saw the clothes burning on the maiden. That took a direct hit. I don't know who hit it.

Frank said when his ship came up the river he looked up the drives and saw a space. His heart dropped and nobody knew where we all were. Some of the neighbours said they were sure we'd been in the shelter. Someone else said, 'Try over the water,' and then he found us all in Grandma Collins' in Molyneux Road.

Anyway there's plenty of room for everyone here. There's a real bathroom like Mag's and two bedrooms and a playroom.

At the moment Gabe and I are sleeping in the playroom because Stan's here, so he's in our bedroom. Stan's Dada's friend and I love him. He's a soldier too. Very early in the mornings I have a bath because I like the real bath. The water's cold but then I hop in with Stan for a warm, and he says, 'Oh God, wet fish.'

Soon I won't be able to sleep with Stan because he's going to marry Elsie. Mama says married people sleep together. Maybe if I marry Gabe I could sleep with Stan.

At the bottom of the garden there's a gate leading to Nine Barrow Down, and an appleblossom tree. Yesterday Gabe and I lay down on the tartan rug, in the hole under the tree and pretended we were dead matchgirls. All the pink above was Heaven and it smelt of blossom and sun and that's what Heaven's like. We fell asleep and Auntie couldn't find us. She went searching all up the hill and found the strawberry punnet with nearly all our picnic finished, dropped on the ground. That was because the adder chased us.

Summer 1944/II

It was lovely last night. Our well's run dry and Dada woke us up and said, 'Come on, we're going for a ride in our nighties! We're going for water to the emergency tap.'

I think it was about eleven o'clock but it was still a bit light and we put all the jerry cans and buckets and jugs and kettles into the car and drove down to the seafront.

I loved the sea last night. It wasn't the same as daytime. The moon made everything beautiful and quiet with no people. When we'd filled up all our cans, Dada pushed us on the swings in our nighties. I think we looked like night fairies.

I didn't want to go home, and Mama had brought a thermos flask and scones, so we sat on the slipway and had a midnight picnic and watched the sea for ever.

September 1944

I'm four.

Mama had made me a beautiful flower chair for my birthday tea. I'm going to sit in the big chair and it's covered all over with flowers and leaves and bows.

It's not quite as flowery as Gabe's was. Gabe's birthday is on 30 April and there are more actual flowers then, because it's spring. On 3 September, you get more berries and leaves, but I still love my chair.

It's going to be a special tea. Mama's made lots of different sandwiches. Egg and apple and dates that Frank brought back. Then butterfly cakes with lemon buttercream. You make the cream with butter and sugar and lemon juice. We couldn't spare the butter so Mama used marge and nobody takes sugar in tea so we have enough. And Dada got a lemon from camp in exchange for some sugar we didn't need. Everything's short. Frank's going to try to bring some oranges home next trip.

Grandad was very pleased last week because Mama sent him two lovely onions home by registered post. She got some from Castles' Farm.

The Castles are coming to my party. Michael's eleven and he takes me for drives on the tractor. The other person is Peter from over the road. They might bring me a present.

I've already had one from Guido. He works on the farm and he made me a wooden doll. He's carved it himself. He goes past our house every day and I have a chat with him but he can't speak English very well. Sometimes Mama gives him a cup of tea and a scone.

Yesterday after he gave me the doll he leaned on the gate over the road, to look at the flowers and the grandma shouted at him: 'Go away, dirty Itiy.'

And then she scrubbed the gate where he'd been. I don't think she likes him.

I've also got a birthday cake with green icing and white writing but the writing's run a bit.

The next day, Monday, the pace of work really began to hot up. We had a readthrough of *Is The Priest At Home?* and spent the morning blocking the moves. In the afternoon we worked on *The Country Boy*.

It was great seeing the whole company together in the second play, with Cecil and Noel bringing their idiosyncrasies into the group.

Cecil had not been idle during the first couple of weeks. He ran the raffle and had been busy preparing boxes of tickets and prizes for the opening night and many thereafter. The drill was to sweep the theatre in the interval selling tickets for a shilling and draw the prizewinner before the curtain went up on Act II. There were to be a few special things on the first night, but basically the daily draw was a bottle of Paddy.

'All you young ones come out in the interval to sell the tickets,' said Cecil.

I didn't fancy that a bit. In my limited experience of the theatre, I had become a great believer in maintaining the mystique, the illusion, and the prospect of traipsing through the audience flogging tickets, before returning to the gentle wistful character of Eileen, filled me with horror. I muttered something about a quick change and hoped Cecil would forget about me.

As we left for lunch, Jim caught me up on the stairs to remind me of my job as décor ASM.

'God, Jim, I've no idea what's required, and no taste,' I said, hoping he'd find a more suitable candidate.

'You'll learn,' said he. 'All you need is to look through the prop store for the older plays, and find some pictures to hang on the wall, little tables and stick a few bits on them.'

'Not too bad.'

'However, for modern, smart stuff for *The Tender Trap* you'll need to borrow from the gift shop or Hilliards. Work out what you want and go in to see them after lunch tomorrow, they're used to it.' Jim grinned, seeing the look of dread on my face.

Having got out of the stage-management so far, I was to grow to loathe my soft option as décor mistress. The torture of bumming around Hilliards begging for nice pictures and smart pieces of occasional furniture hung over me. I had to do this every day, you see. Different plays. Collect them and take them back. There was the horror too of going in some days to collect a picture or a lamp that everyone had got used to, only to find it had been sold, or the embarrassment of returning a pretty firescreen with a stain on it where some enthusiastic thespian had chucked his 'whiskey' in the action. Hilliards were really tolerant though. We gave them a huge credit in the programme, and the family themselves were loyal supporters of the theatre.

For those of us who lived at New Street, the pattern of the day was dominated by the wonderful meals that Cis put on for us. It was funny to go 'home' for lunch. It was paid for and none of us could afford to miss it. We'd usually have a quick drink in O'Leary's and then scatter down the road as Sal dished up.

Lunch-times were enlivened by the presence of the three gardaí from the station next door, who took the midday meal with the sisters. The big table was filled by all of us so they were crammed on a little one against the window.

These were the days before policemen were ever called pigs. When they were still just somebody's sons, very young, away from home, making a living and a life like the rest of us. We'd sometimes see them at the dances, gauche without the trappings of office, in brown suits with slicked-back hair.

John McMahon used to tease them. 'Caught any crooks today? Who's minding the shop while you're here?'

I never remember seeing any other policemen. There must have been a sergeant, I suppose, but with the full muster of the force wading into Cis's grub, twelve-thirty to one-thirty would have been the ideal time for a bank job.

Towards the end of the week, Maggie and I decided we needed a break from work and we'd take up the invitation from the boys to go to the Europa one night. We'd soon be locked in to the carousel of performance hours and find it hard to mix with anybody working a normal day.

We met Dan and Eamonn in the Grand after dinner (I've always been a cheap date) and we drove through the summer evening to the hotel. We were surprised when we got inside how nice it was; quite Scandinavian in design, lots of beams and wood and sloping ceilings.

As usual I felt wrongly dressed. I've never managed to quite hit the spot with clothes. I'm either hopelessly overdressed or unchicly casual. I'd worn a smart but rather stiff yellow suit, one I'd bought as part of the wardrobe one is required to furnish by Equity rules. My shoes were too high – my skirt too long. I felt a real prat! Hey ho. Maggie on the other hand wore jeans and a sweater and looked terrific and at ease. I didn't have any jeans. I don't know why. Just rather boring trousers.

It soon became evident that this upstairs bar of the Europa was the hub of social life for the comparatively affluent young of Killarney. As the place filled up, we were introduced to loads of people, all very charming and attractive, but a different kind of gang from the crowd at the Sunday dances.

I felt a bit out of it. Maybe it was the stiff yellow suit, maybe it was that old feeling of not being one of the 'in' crowd. I felt too that we were objects of curiosity, two English actresses, out for the night with the local talent.

It was also a kind of Ireland with which I was not familiar. In my brief time there I'd come to love a town where you could enjoy whole nights in a pub with a pint of Guinness and sing yourself hoarse. Here in the Europa the 'sophisticated' society I thought I wanted made me feel uncomfortable and gauche.

My own paranoia apart, we didn't have a bad night and around 10 p.m. we set off for a slow drive home through the shadowy hills. We all moderately fancied each other. Maybe Dan and I marginally more than Maggie and Eamonn. Dan stopped the car by the 18th hole of the golf course, obviously a favourite spot of the fellers, and we spent a happy hour in the damp green, indulging in good old-fashioned heavy petting, fighting our way through tight suits, yellow and brown. It was a friendly end to the evening, not entirely satisfactory for the boys, Maggie and I remaining resolutely virgo intacta, par for the course, I'm sure, in Catholic Ireland. But they were good sports and dropped me at the door of New Street, flushed and rumpled with my suspenders in a twist.

'Good night. Thanks.'

'See ya again.'

The gang were still up having supper, big hunks of bread and cheese, slices of onion and jam.

'How was the cream of Killarney society?' John McMahon, challenging behind his glasses.

'Fine. Lovely night.'

But he knew. 'You'll be much too busy for gadding soon. Rehearsing all day and playing at night.'

'Yes.' I sat in a chair, smoothing my yellow suit and picking bits of grass off it.

'18th hole?' said Kitty.

I blushed.

'Here, I made you a cheese and onion sandwich.'

Liam. Loving Liam.

'Thanks, treas.'

Autumn 1944

Yesterday I got on the wrong bus going home. I knew it was the wrong bus because it wasn't my driver. It was a serious driver, not a smiling one and there weren't enough people on it. My bus has a lot of people and leaves quite soon. But this one took a long time.

I got on it because a big girl said, 'That's your bus,' very certainly. When it started to move along the roads I looked out and didn't recognize anywhere. There were too many houses and my stomach churned. After a while I went and said: 'You're not my driver.'

And the driver looked puzzled. He stopped the bus and tried to work out where I live.

'Lower Valley Road.'

But he couldn't go there.

I didn't know what to do but then a kind big girl said I could go home with her and sort it out.

I had a lovely tea and her mother had a telephone and rang school and Mama was very worried when I didn't come home, but then Dada came in Smiler Miles's car and took me home, because his is broken.

Last night we saw Father Christmas and he breathed on us. We were frightened. Mama kept telling us to go to sleep or Father Christmas wouldn't come. We had Dada's big socks laid out on the end of our beds. And we kept closing our eyes but we weren't tired so we shouted for a cup of cocoa. Mama gave us one and then we had to go to sleep so we were quiet for a bit, then we started laughing and Mama came in and said she was sick and tired and Father Christmas would know about us being naughty and not come.

We were still chatting and singing when suddenly I heard bells and heavy footsteps outside the playroom door in the garden. We lay as still as mice. My stomach turned over and my heart was jumping. The footsteps came into the room and right up to the bed and we could hear rustling and lumps on our feet. I just opened my eye a tiny bit and then I saw him – I saw his boots and his red coat and his white beard and he was breathing loudly.

When he'd gone Gabe and I didn't move. We lay perfectly still and not a sound. After a while Mama and Auntie came in.

'Are you all right?'

'He's been,' I said.

'He breathed on us,' said Gabe.

'Don't you want to see what he brought?'

'No.'

'Well let's have a look.'

'Ooh look,' said Mama. 'Pot dolls.'

'Pot dolls.'

She put one each under the covers for us to cuddle.

'See the rest in the morning. Good night and God bless you.'

46

It was very quiet.

'Come on, Paul, they've gone to sleep now. Let's open our presents.'

Opening night was suddenly upon us. We had a dress rehearsal on Monday afternoon, and hung about fussing in the big communal dressing-rooms, tidying our places, ironing our clothes, muttering our lines. There was one room for men and one for women but lots of toing and froing between the two. I think actors are very reluctant to leave the theatre on the day of a first night in case they break the spell by leaving the building.

I was extremely nervous, I hadn't been on a stage since my first job at Windsor and although Jim had constantly reassured me, I had severe doubts that I could 'project' past the fourth row. Funny thing projection. It's more than just a loud voice or good articulation. It's something more ephemeral; it's an ability to shoot your spirit like a boomerang to the very furthest corners of the theatre. You only know you've done it when the boomerang comes back.

We finished dinner about 6.30 p.m., a meal I could hardly touch that night, and I walked through the town with John McMahon. All along the way people stopped us.

'Good luck now.'

'Have a great night.'

'Good luck. Knock 'em dead.'

'I'm coming to see you on Wednesday.'

We were part of this place. Everyone knew us. It was an odd feeling to have a whole town behind you. I suppose along with the souvenir shops, the jaunting cars and the lakes, we were a fairly major attraction for the summer season.

At 8.50 p.m. Vincent called the five – five minutes until the curtain up. I'd been ready since seven-thirty. The 9.00 p.m. start was to allow the visitors to finish

47

their sight-seeing and have a meal before going to the theatre.

At Beginners I went on to the stage to get in place at the stove. I was first on in the play. From behind the curtain I could hear the anticipatory buzz of a full house. Then the wave of hush as the lights went down and Vincent slowly brought in the music – the first bars of 'Misa Eire' by Sean O'Riada. That music somehow transported me, then and always, lifted me out of my leaden fear and on to the angel's wing of a good night. Nobody quite knows why one night is 'good' and another 'bad'. Why one audience is with us and another against. We say the same words in more or less the same way. But the audience takes on a homogeneous soul and responds to a man either very well or not so well to what we do.

On a bad night it's the embarrassment of a blind date when nobody fancies each other. On a good, it's like a great meal with wonderful companions. On a great night it's falling in love, that unexplainable conjoining of spirits so close, that we breathe together. For me that first night was one such night.

I knew I'd be OK. I could feel the curiosity and warmth in the house and by the time I had my first exchange with Liam, I knew I could do it.

As the first half closed, Cecil came up, calling for us to get out into the house and sell raffle tickets.

'I can't, Cecil. I feel sick. Got to go to the loo.'

He gave up after a couple more tries.

In the dressing-room we were elated as we drank our tea. Every character grabbed the audience's attention. It was, as Jim knew of old, a sure-fire hit, a crowd pleaser that appealed both to the local population, and the Yanks. I looked around the room at all of us; at Pat, round and shining, Jim, in his element, grinning from ear to ear. And felt a huge wave of joy. To be there in that country, doing what I wanted, and doing it quite well.

Never in my wildest dreams did I ever think a life in the theatre would come to me so soon and so perfectly.

As the play drew to a close, I had my little song to sing, sitting on a stool in the corner. John McMahon was right. Not a dry eye in the house! On this night there was a pin-drop silence and then applause. Some nights only the silence. I didn't mind either way. I loved that feeling of holding the audience in my arms.

After the curtain and the really great reception, we all ganged into the Grand where the schooners of sherry sailed in like galleons. In the course of the evening I dropped a cigarette into my sherry. And put it on the radiator to dry. Towards the end of the night, I lit up and smoked it. I flew round the room, hit the ceiling and touched Heaven's gate before turning several shades of green. It was a rare kind of high, never to be repeated.

The New Street crowd took me home and Joan aimed me into bed where I lay knocked out till a latish rehearsal call the next day.

Early Summer 1945

We're back home again, now. In Radnor Drive. When they kept talking about going home at the end of the war, I wasn't quite sure where home really was, but I know this is home because it felt right when we got into 'Lime Street'.

I thought we were going to stay at Heathfields for a long long time but suddenly the Castles wanted it back. Mama was crying and tired and there was a dreadful lot of cleaning and packing to do, and we kept wanting our dinner, so I went to stay with Mag for a couple of days, with Mama's little brown case. But Gabe stayed and she was whingeing while Mama was trying to clear up, but Mag couldn't have us both. Only me, because I'm no trouble.

Anyway in the end everything was cleared out and packed and this morning we got up very early. Mama had everything ready last night but she still had to run around a lot, doing last-minute things. And Dada was quite cross in case we missed the train.

'Come on, Nora, you'll give me a heart attack.'

Because he had the car already going and the starting handle was juddering, Dada didn't come with us. He's going to put everything in the car and drive up. But he took us to Bournemouth for the London train.

The first part of the journey was OK because Dada settled us in and found a carriage with just another lady in it. But when we got to London we had to get a taxi to Euston and there were thousands of people all going for trains.

I carried my own case but Gabe started whingeing because Mama had to put the other bags in the pushchair and we held on and ran along the platform to get a carriage when the train pulled in. When the doors started opening, Mama said: 'Quick, I'll get a seat. You stay there and mind Gabe.'

And she put Gabe in the pushchair and sat me on a case while she ran into the train with some other bags to grab a seat. And I didn't want to stay on my own minding Gabe, and I shouted: 'You know, it's not right to leave a child of this age with all this responsibility.'

When she came back to put us in the carriage I felt better, because she spread rugs over the seats and made it like a house, and there was a little pull-down table so we put our colouring books and pencils on it, like a desk.

Then Mama put out the first picnic in the strawberry punnet next to me and I started with a sandwich.

A couple of people looked in for seats but Mama said we made the carriage look quite full and put them off.

One man sat with us for bit but he didn't like my hairy molly. I had it in a jar with leaves and after it had eaten its lunch I let it out for a run. He tutted and muttered about 'Children under control' but Mama went on settling Gabe down to sleep and started to tell us 'The Little Matchgirl' again. Then the man went.

Suddenly all the doors started slamming and whistles

blowing and I smelled the beautiful smell of the steam starting up, and then we were off very slowly. The train made dreadful noises and screeched as it started up. I don't think it was oiled properly.

I looked out of the window and watched the arches go past counting them. Just as I got to four, the door near our carriage was opened and a kit-bag thrown into the corridor. A sailor was running along with the train, trying to get on. Mama jumped up and grabbed his hand and yanked him into the corridor and he fell in and started laughing and they managed to haul the door closed.

He came and sat with us and didn't mind my hairy molly or the clutter.

Mama asked him a lot of questions about the Atlantic Approaches. He didn't know Frank but he'd been torpedoed too and got out safe in the lifeboats. Like Frank.

I love trains. I think I've been on them a lot before but I was too small to appreciate it.

When you go by in a train you can see things for a long while when you look back, like a man in a field, putting a big bucket of pigswill out for the pigs; I waved to him but he didn't wave back.

I love the dunkada-dunk dunkada-dunk noise that the train makes and the lovely smutty smell when the steam blows.

After a while we had another picnic and we gave the sailor some because he didn't have any dinner and he gave Gabe and me half a banana each. I remember having that before but Gabe didn't like it, and spat it out. So Mama finished it.

When you're on a train it feels like a bit of a dream because all the places go by but you can't touch them or pick the flowers.

I played a game of trying to read the station names when they went by very fast. If it was a long station, it was a bit easier because you had a few chances.

One thing I didn't like about the train was when I had to cross the joining bit between carriages, because the lav was on

51

the other side, I thought I might fall down the joining-up pieces and get trapped. It's got a soft piece in the middle and you have to sort of jump across.

The first time I went with Mama, but then a bit later on I went by myself and my stomach was churning but I made it. Another time I waited for the train to slow down and only just finished when we pulled into Stafford. It's against the law to do it when the train's standing in the station and I hurried quickly back to our carriage in case the guard caught me.

It was raining in Stafford. 'The Midlands, sodden and unkind,' said Mama and then two more people got into our carriage and I fell asleep.

I woke up going through a tunnel and it was very dark and noisy, but even when we came out of the tunnel it was dark and Gabe started to cry because she was frightened. I was too, but I didn't show it. Mama said there were no lights because of the blackout. I told Gabe we couldn't have lights on in case the Germans bombed the train, but that didn't really make her feel better because she started to cry about the bombs.

'Change at Crewe. Change at Crewe.'

I suddenly felt excited, I remembered 'Change at Crewe' from another time.

'I think we're nearly there, Gabe. This is "Change at Crewe". Nearly there.'

Mama said she was going to hop off and get the thermos flask filled up. I didn't want her to go.

'It's all right, lovie, there's nearly quarter of an hour here.'

There were lots of lights in the station and the lady in our carriage said: 'Don't worry, your mum'll be back in a minute.'

So everything was all right and I started to tell Gabe what we were going to have for dinner when we got home. But suddenly the train lurched and clanked and I ran into the corridor.

'Mum, Mama, they're going without you.'

But I couldn't see her, and so I jumped on to the platform to find the guard.

'Don't go. My Mama's not on.'

And the lady in our carriage was holding Gabe and shouting: 'It's all right, they're only shunting engines.'

Then suddenly I saw Mama and everything was OK. And we hopped back on together. After a bit I fell asleep again.

All of a sudden we were there.

'Liverpool Lime Street. Liverpool Lime Street!'

I woke up. I smelt the home smell and all the voices sounded of home. A porter lifted me down: 'There y'are now, chick.'

And then I saw Maurice.

'Mau, here we are.' And I ran all the way along the platform to give him a hug.

We took a taxi through the tunnel and Mau said it went right under the Mersey, to save you getting the ferry. It was beautiful in the tunnel. Lots of orange lights but I was quite worried about if there was a hole that the water would get in and drown us.

We're home now. Auntie's made us a lovely ham salad and Grandad's going to let me sleep in his bed tonight.

'You're the best girl in forty streets.'

'And me, Grandad,' says Gabe.

'And you're the best in thirty-nine. Come on, chickadees, I'll tell you a story.'

After Grandad's gone and the light's out, I'll lie in bed and listen to the foghorns on the river. I love that sound. I love it because it makes me feel very near to the water, as if I'm on it. Sometimes though, it makes me very sad and I almost cry because it's a very lonely sound.

From then on our lives became very regular and disciplined; playing every night, gradually rehearsing more plays until we had a repertoire that afforded a change of programme every night.

It's amazing the capacity the human brain has for

storing stuff. I was walking round that town with seven plays in my head by midsummer, big parts in all of them, throwing the right switch on the right night seven days a week.

Because of the energy I was using I grew very thin during the first half of the season. Around six stone eight or nine, Pat recommended Guinness as a good body-builder, so I abandoned my sherry and piled into halves of draft Guinness at O'Leary's bar. I can't believe I ever drank sherry, and in such quantities!

It's funny for me to look back now and remember how much of our social life centred round the bars of Killarney. I don't drink alcohol now, and feel a bit out of place in a pub, but then O'Leary's, in the main street, was like a second home for us all. We gradually abandoned the Grand as being a bit too posh. Some people drank at the Arbutus but mostly in the daytime we were to be found playing darts and at night squashed into the snug. This was a curious little window corner that, at night, was partitioned off with a wooden door, for ladies to drink in. Mrs O'Leary was very firm about this. After a certain hour, ladies did not drink at the bar. So our group were hustled into the hens' corner – with our accompanying men. I sometimes had a great urge to defy the tradition and play darts stark naked in the public bar. But Pat restrained me, reminding me that she had to come back next year!

At the end of my first six weeks I opened an account at the *Oifig an Phoist* and deposited £12, not bad on £8.10s.0d. a week.

Nobody spent a great deal. We didn't have the time for one thing, and secondly we couldn't really afford it. None of us knew what followed this lovely long job. Our entertainments were very simply – the pub or the Sunday dance. Later in the season with free time in the days, we'd hire a bike or one of the jarveys' horses to go riding.

John McMahon was right about Dan and Eamonn. We

didn't have time for the 'in' crowd and after a couple more dates with them, Maggie and I called it a day by mutual consent.

Like any group of people working together over a prolonged period, friendships waxed and waned and gradually little groups formed who had more in common than others.

Throughout the season the New Street bunch remained very close. We all liked each other and after my initial feeling that John didn't really care for the young ones, he became my friend, my ally, even my admirer. I think he really liked working with me and trusted me. For my part I think he was a great actor, up there with the knights. His range was terrific, he could make you roar with laughter, or devastate you with a tragedy. I'll never know why he didn't move beyond the summer season and winter fit-ups. Maybe something in himself didn't want to. Maybe it was safe to return year after year to New Street and sparring with Kitty.

Joan had a room, just a half-landing down from mine, and I felt I knew her from the first week. She was always good to talk to, and we shared a lot in common in the way of hopes and dreams. I found out her boyfriend was Jewish and her mother didn't approve of this match. It seemed an awful waste of a love sacrificed at the altar of parental opinion.

Liam underwent a metamorphosis as the season went on. Pat Turner and Jim had had a long-term relationship which might have ended in marriage but didn't. I met them as they were personally breaking up but professionally still having to run a company together. Into this came Liam, a very shy man in his thirties, who hadn't had much in the way of girlfriends, and suddenly found that he and Pat were soul mates. It was a relationship that did a great deal for both of them. It restored Pat's faith in men and made Liam into a more self-confident and forthright person.

As the younger members of the company, Maggie and Vincent and Tony and I tended to be a group in the beginning. We almost always went to the dances on Sunday nights; didn't necessarily stay together. It was an easy relationship like having two good brothers who didn't tease you.

Some days we'd hire bikes and ride off into the countryside, ending up at one of the lakes, for a picnic, and arrive back in time for a tea with Mrs B at the café.

After we'd been there a few times, we noticed that each visit our bills got smaller. We'd give her say six shillings for four teas and get four shillings change, depending on if the boss was there or not. And we'd have had huge teas with mountains of everything. It was embarrassing but wonderful for our puny finances. Once when she actually gave me 5s 6d change from 6s I said, 'Mrs B, you can't keep doing this.'

She whispered, 'Don't worry, I'll get it off the Americans.'

I don't think she really stung anybody badly, just the odd threepence here and there, taking from the rich to give to the poor. Us!

The Americans came in droves to Killarney, many of them searching for their roots. The US has always been proud of the blood line that came from Ireland, giving the huge new country poets, politicians and policemen! And with the Kennedy presidency there was a massive upsurge of interest in all things Irish, which was reciprocated when Kennedy visited Ireland that summer. The papers were filled with the visit, all the more appreciated because it was after the loss of their baby, Patrick. The whole of Ireland mourned with them.

This was the beginning of the sixties and the other big news of the day was the Profumo Scandal. Christine Keeler and Mandy Rice-Davies became the most photographed exponents of the swinging sixties. I wouldn't say they were exactly role models for me, but as my lingering virginity loomed ever larger in my mind, I couldn't help envying their sang-froid. They looked fantastic, mini-skirted, smiling – Mandy always the chic one – Christine a bit more dishevelled. Neither of them the least embarrassed at being the most celebrated courtesans in England.

(I met Christine Keeler a couple of years later at The Pheasantry in Chelsea, not that she would remember me. She was not a beautiful girl, but she did have a great sweetness and an extraordinary charisma about her. She invited me to a party but I was too nervous to go – didn't know where it might take me – coward!)

But in Killarney, Mary Quant and Vidal Sassoon were still unknown and though miniskirts were beginning to climb up towards the bum, for me the most desired item of clothing was a pair of jeans.

I drew a couple of pounds out of the *Oifig an Phoist* and combed the town (a matter of twenty minutes at the outside), for a really sexy pair of jeans. In my mind's eye I saw myself looking a bit like Brigitte Bardot in tight, faded, blue denim with a Levi label. I looked in vain. The stately aisles of Hilliards had no such garments. I settled in the end for a rather dark blue pair, not particularly tight, not even necessarily denim. It was a start. I lived in those jeans that summer – 21s 6d.

Spring 1946

There's going to be a May Procession for Our Lady's birthday and someone's going to be the May Queen. I hope it's me. You wear a beautiful long frock and have blue bows in your hair if you're the May Queen. Even if you're only a handmaiden you wear blue bows, but only a short frock. Then the Queen and the handmaidens walk all round the grounds at St Peter and Paul's till they get to the throne – then she gets a beautiful crown.

57

Mama says don't get too excited. Don't be disappointed if I'm not chosen this year because my hair's a bit short.

It had to be cut short because of the livestock. I kept tearing at my hair. One day when I was sitting behind Kay I saw little white beetles walking up her ringlets. She's got beautiful shiny ringlets and pink slides.

I told Mama when I got home and she got her tin-bath cleaning face, and she fine-toothcombed my hair for a long time until I was really fed up and tired. And she found lots of beetles. And then she washed my hair in green soft soap. Auntie got a special thing from her school nurse and everyone put some on. Everyone had cream on their hair except Grandad. He didn't have enough hair. In the end she had to cut it short for safety so no more beetles could jump on to my hair.

Frank came home and said: 'What in the name of God have you done to her? She wasn't this plain.'

I'm not, just the hair.

Who do you think was chosen for the May Queen? Kay – she didn't have her ringlets cut off.

Battersea 1946

We're in Battersea now. Dada's got a London teaching job again.

I first saw the park when our taxi crossed the river. It only took a couple of seconds going over Chelsea Bridge.

'That's the River Thames,' said Dada. It's not very big and no shore. No room for a ferry at all. 'It goes a very long way. It's much wider near the sea. Look! There's Pulfords where you can have a cup of tea and a bun.'

He showed us a kind of red hut on wheels with a little flap-down along one side and a man was handing tea and sandwiches through the flap. I wanted to stop but Dada said we'd arrived and then he showed us the drive and the swings. The swings looked a bit small, nothing like our fairground and all grey, no colours.

And then we saw the drive. Out of the taxi window I could see huge trees all in a row along the edge of the drive, and a very long road, very flat, not sloping like Radnor.

Our flat is huge, everything is on one floor.

You go in the entrance and up four lots of stairs and there you are.

When you come in the front door there are two big rooms on the left and the second one is for Gabe and me. It has french windows on to a balcony and we can see the park.

Opposite our room is the kitchen and that has a little back balcony where there's a lift for the rubbish and an outside lav.

Then if you go right at the front door there's a very long corridor and first a little bedroom, then the bathroom, then two big bedrooms and a very tiny bedroom at the end. There are also two closets, one's huge and you can hide in there.

Maurice is going to live with us so he'll have one of the big bedrooms and Hilda might stay a year, so there'll be room for her too. But Mama says we can have one of the little rooms as a playroom sometimes.

We haven't got much furniture, mostly beds, and the two blue uncut moquette armchairs from Radnor.

We've got a table for the kitchen but no chairs so Mama's making stools from the tea-chests that the removal man left. She's made two so far and I'm helping her. She's painted them cream and padded the lids with lots of sacking and covered them with bits of old flowered curtain. They look lovely.

When we'd finished all our work Dada lit a fire in the front room and we had cheese and celery and bread and butter and listened to Saturday Night Theatre. *The coal is in a kind of cupboard in the kitchen but you need coke for the boiler so Dada's going to make a space on the balcony for that.*

We've got a bed settee in the front room as well. It's bright red, with wooden arms, but Mama's thrown a rug over it because she says it's a bit too red. It's utility. She calls it 'Red Joe'.

Dada took us to the swings just along the road. Now we know where they are we can go on our own. They're just inside the park by the main gate. They're all iron, and when you go in there's a funny smell, a bit dirty, but all the different things are very good. I like the ropes best. You put your elbow through a chain loop and run very hard till you're off the ground and then you keep going by doing a little run every time you hit the ground. There are different lengths according to how tall you are, but you've got to be careful that the danglers don't hit you in the eye or a big girl doesn't go too fast and kick you.

I was trying to jump on the little roundabout, dragging on the handles to make it stop, and a big girl pushed me away.

'Shove off, you're posh.'

There's a sandpit too but we're not allowed to go in there.

While Mama and Dada were distempering the walls in the kitchen, I asked her if these were our walls and she said they were Battersea Borough Council's but as good as ours for a very long time.

'Can I write on them?'

'Yes.'

So I wrote 'Pauline Angela Collins' by the boiler and drew a house and then I drew a tree on the Welsh dresser, and Mama said: 'Shall we leave it there?'

But I said 'no' and she let me distemper over it.

And afterwards Gabe and I helped Dada paint the bookcase.

I hope we stay here for a very long while.

After about nine weeks we had a good repertoire of plays under our belts and the days were free after the ten o'clock fit-up. Maggie immediately hired a bike and systematically 'did' the surrounding countryside. I didn't feel so energetic and was really quite happy just 'being', walking the town, wandering in the demesne or just sitting in the sun in the graveyard.

One day, strolling back towards New Street, I heard someone shout my name. There was Tony in the door of O'Leary's.

'Come and have a jar.'

'I'm just going to lunch. Cis'll have it ready.'

'Well, come for a ride this afternoon then.'

'Bike?'

'Horse.'

'Horse!'

'Well, pony.'

'I can't ride.' Dim memories of ambling along on a French cart-horse.

'Yes, you can. It's just the jarveys' ponies – they'll rent a couple to us. Meet me at two-thirty by the jaunting cars.'

'I'll be no good.'

'Try it.' Tony, grinning and persuasive, hard to resist.

'OK.'

At three o'clock I found myself, in my jeans, jogging lumpenly up and down on the back of a square pony who deeply resented being ridden on his day off. We were heading for the lakeshore at Castle Island, Tony leading, me behind. Danny, who'd hired us the ponies had jambled a few unintelligible instructions at us about commands to stop and go, but basically we were in uncharted territory. As far as we could make out 'giddy-up' and 'whoa now' were the key words, and a pull on the reins left and right more or less had us turning corners.

Sometimes, however, my 'Micky' didn't want to 'whoa' at all, and sometimes he would stop abruptly of his own volition to munch a bit of grass, to smell the air or sometimes apparently just for a bit of a think. However, we gradually got to understand each other, mainly by my not giving him any commands at all, capitulation for me being the better part of valour.

I was glad to get off when we reached the lakeshore and tied up the ponies while we sat on the brackeny banks and watched the lake. The afternoon was completely silent. The birds even were still, holding their breath till the water moved again.

'Wouldn't it be wonderful to stay here for ever?'

'Do you mean here, in this moment?' said Tony, leaning across to pick a biscuit from the packet. 'Or here in this country?'

I looked at him, surprised at how exactly he'd arrowed into my thoughts.

'Well, I was enchanted by the moment but actually, I do love this country. I feel right here. I have been thinking if it would be possible to stay.'

'And work?'

'Yes.'

'Well, you'll have your Irish Equity card soon. Maybe we should have a look at Dublin at the end of the season.'

'Where though? How do you begin?'

'There's quite a bit of work in Telefis, small parts in the series.'

'What about the theatre?'

'Fair amount I think. We'll ask Pat and Jim.'

'John McMahon says there are a few touring companies in the winter. Some quite good. What about that?'

'Wouldn't that be a bit sad after Killarney?'

'I don't know.' I looked past him out at the lake. 'It would depend on who I was with, on the crowd you know.'

We sat a bit in a silence and then by some mutual consent both lay flat on our backs looking at the uncertain sky.

Micky pierced the peace by snorting and rearing at some invisible enemy and by the time he'd calmed down, it was raining. Persistent Irish rain. Soft, insidious Irish rain. We set off back home along the wooded banks of a little stream, to shelter a bit from the wet. As John O'Hara once wrote, 'The horse knows the way', and Micky was doing fine without a word from me, until

Tony, in a sudden fit of equestrian enthusiasm, giddy-uped his mount into a gallopy trot. All at once Micky's tired old ears pricked up to the giddy-up and he shot forward on Tony's command into a thunderous lopsided gallop that had me clinging to his head and dodging the overhanging branches. We zoomed past Tony and no amount of 'whoas' on my part could slow him down.

Tony caught me up and shouted, 'Whoa', in a deep, Kerry voice. Micky stopped dead, old chauvinist that he was. I realized then that these ponies only ever listen to men's voices and my twitterings were like a foreign language to him.

We lolloped back, damp and giggling, and fell into Mrs B's café for tea. No one else there.

'Just the two of you?'

'Yep. Just us.'

'Tea for two. All right so. And two for tea.' She hummed as she shuffled into the back.

'Good day, eh?' Tony, combing back the damp hair.

'Despite the jigs and the reels. I think I'd better ride a bike next time though.'

I'm rubbing my knees, smelling my hands. 'And my lovely jeans smell of Micky.'

Autumn 1946

I love this new school. We go with Mama on the 137 bus over Chelsea Bridge to Sloane Square. The first few times Mama took us right into the school but now she leaves us at the top of Cadogan Street, and we walk down with all the other children. Then she hops quickly back on the bus to go to her school, because she's gone back to teaching now to pay for things.

Eventually we'll be able to go on our own because I'm quite sensible and I could be in charge of Gabe if she doesn't fight with me.

Last week we had a fight and she bit me on the bottom and drew blood.

We have a uniform at this school, a cherry hat a bit like a sailor's beret, a grey coat in winter and a grey skirt with straps and a cream blouse.

There's a shop called Daniel Neal where you have to buy these things or you can buy a pattern and make them. Mama bought our berets and coats but she made everything else, including our gym skirts and ballet frocks, all from the same pattern. I thought ballet frocks would be white and flouncy, but they're duck-egg blue and quite plain.

I'm not very good at ballet yet. I wobble quite a lot when I'm on one leg and the one off the ground feels too heavy.

'Beef to the heels like a Mullingar heifer,' says Mama.

I think I have the best teacher in this school. Sister Teresa Joseph lets you go on to the next book even if you're not meant to have finished so soon, so you don't get fed up waiting.

We're doing nature this week. Everyone brought a jam jar and Sister gave us some blotting-paper and a bean and that'll grow into a little plant. We've got our names on them and we have to keep the blotting-paper damp.

Next week we start silkworms.

Christmas Eve 1946

Home again at Radnor Drive. It's funny but Wallasey still feels home although we really live in London now, I suppose. Anyway, we're here for all of Christmas, nearly a month.

We did a lovely play on the window sill. It's big enough to stand on and you can draw the curtains. I was Our Lady and Little Phil was St Joseph, and Gabe was the Angel Gabriel. Marg was Baby Jesus, but Little Phil kept laughing when she put two fingers in her mouth, to suck. At the end, we all sang 'Away In A Manger' and everyone clapped.

Then everybody got round the piano and sang carols. I love

that. Then someone said: 'Little Phil, sing "Silent Night",'
because he's got the best voice.

And he said 'No', and everyone said: 'Come on, Phil.'

And he still said 'No'. Then Uncle Phil said: 'You will
sing "Silent Night".'

And Little Phil cried and said he wouldn't and then he got
sent into the bedroom. I don't think that was fair. Nobody
asked me. I wanted to sing 'Come To The Manger' but
nobody asked. Probably because I haven't got the best
voice.

Anyway it was all forgotten by Christmas morning.

Mama spent her whole first month's salary. She bought
beautiful presents for everyone from a big shop in London
called Harrods.

Dada was a bit fed up. He said: 'Champagne tastes on a
beer income.'

Grandad said: 'She's always been flockhoolack.'

Mama said: 'Never mind. If you've got it, spend it. When
you haven't, don't.'

We had lovely things from Father Christmas but the very
best present was from Frank.

Two huge rocking horses, a white one for me and Gabe,
and a green one for Phil and Marg. When you get on them,
it's like a real horse and you can pretend you're riding away
to a foreign land.

Frank bought them in Calcutta in India and he and Alan
Peters and two other sailors carried them all the way down
Chowringhi Lane because they couldn't find a taxi.

I love Christmas.

The next day on my way to the chemist, I saw Declan
unloading carcasses into the butchers. He was between
the lorry and the shop when I went up to say hello. He
was embarrassed and shuffled from one foot to the other,
a great side of beef on his shoulder.

'I'm a bit of a sight,' he said, aimlessly brushing his
overalls with his free hand.

'You're OK.' I felt sorry for his discomfort. 'Do you still want to come on a picnic?'

'Well – I don't know.'

'I wouldn't know how to contact you. Where do you live? Is there a phone?'

'No, no phone. I don't know.'

'Well, I know. Let's say next Sunday, twelve-thirty. By the jaunting cars. We'll get bikes.'

'All right so.' Declan was scarlet and sweating from the great lump on his shoulder and the unbridled curiosity of the passers-by.

'OK. See you Sunday.'

I went off to the chemist and bought Pond's Dream-flower talc and soap, to dust the smell of meat from my nostrils.

As Sunday came near I began to regret my invitation a bit, not because I didn't want to see him, but because I'd promised him a gang and a good time and I wasn't quite sure who would fit in with him best. I decided Liam would be ideal because he was gentle and compassionate and Maggie would be fun and stimulating. I wanted Pat to come but she had a lunch date. Vincent was seeing a town girl and would play it by ear, maybe come, maybe not. For some reason I didn't ask Tony. I just felt he'd somehow frighten Declan or wrongfoot him without meaning to. Tony was very straight, very direct, and had a way of asking you a question that made you feel exposed and vulnerable. I didn't feel Declan could cope with that. He was so much a' ne I felt he needed a gentle introduction into the giddy world of sociability.

On Sunday Cis made us a beautiful picnic – ham, tomato and cheese, egg, mayonnaise, apple pie and flasks of tea and coffee.

At the last moment Kitty liked the look of it all and decided to join us. We all walked up to the bike shop and hired machines, some with baskets, and Liam brought some beer and lemonade.

We sloped round the corner and there was Declan, standing by the jaunting cars in his tight suit and holding a bunch of flowers.

'Aah, God love 'im,' said Liam.

I felt a wave of conflicting emotions, affection, compassion, irritation and exhaustion! The latter because I felt it was going to be an uphill struggle to make it a good occasion. I felt like a society hostess who's got to entertain a foreign ambassador.

'Here we all are.' I introduced all around, although Declan had seen the others before.

'Have ye no bike, Declan?' said Liam.

'No.'

'Get up on the back of mine then.'

Declan handed me the flowers and straddled Liam's back bar uncertainly.

'These are beautiful, Declan, thanks.' I gave him a smile to cheer him on and away we went towards the lakeshore.

'Don't we look ridiculous,' I shouted. 'We look like the Famous Five.'

In some way the wobbly ride broke the ice a bit and by the time we landed, Declan was looking less self-conscious.

It was a chilly day so I asked him to help make a fire while we unpacked the food. He collected wood with Kitty and soon they had a great fire going by the water's edge.

As we laid out Cis's stuff on the cloth, Declan reached in his pocket and came up with a brown packet.

'A little contribution to the table.' Two thick rounds of lamb sandwich.

'Great, Declan. Did your mother make them?'

'No, Mammy was not herself today. She was in a bad humour that I was to be out for the Sunday roast.'

'But you came.'

'I did.' Oh brave one, defying the mammy.

'Thanks, Declan.'

He smiled and we all busied ourselves with the food.

After lunch and a couple of beers, Liam started to sing a rebel song and soon we were all at it, working our way through the Dubliners' stuff, traditional ballads, bringing tears to the eyes.

'"The Gaels, the Gaels of Ireland,"' said Kitty. '"The men that God made mad. For all their wars are merry and all their songs are sad." G. K. Chesterton.'

'Will I sing ye a song?' said Declan suddenly. 'It is a sad song.'

'Yes, go on Declan.'

And so he sang in a voice that stopped the breath, 'She Moved Through the Fair'.

> My young love said to me,
> 'My mother won't mind
> And my father won't slight you
> For your lack of kind.'
> And she stepped away from me
> And this she did say,
> 'It will not be long, love,
> Till our wedding day.'
>
> She stepped away from me
> And she moved through the fair,
> And so fondly I watched her
> Move here and move there.
> She went her way slowly
> With one star awake,
> As the swan in the evening
> Moves over the lake.
>
> The people were saying
> That no two yet wed,
> But the one had a sorrow
> And the other were dead.
> She stepped away from me

With her goods and her gear,
And that was the last
That I saw of my dear.

Last night she came to me,
My dead love came in,
And so softly she moved
That her feet made no din.
She laid her hand on me
And this she did say,
'It will not be long, love,
Till our wedding day.'

That afternoon by the lake was the first time I heard that ballad, and I have yet to hear it better sung. We were all crying when he stopped and I think that made him embarrassed.

'It's just a song.'

'It was beautiful, Declan. Will you teach it to me?'

'Sure.' He climbed up from the ground and stood more formally with his hands by his side. 'Will we walk a bit now?'

'Yes, let's do that.'

We moved in step along the edge of the lake.

'I like the crowd. They're great.'

'I knew you would. Come again if you want.'

'I would like that and maybe too,' he stopped a moment and watched his feet pave the way, 'maybe one day we might go it alone?'

He quite amazed me then. Just when I thought we had, as a group, made him a bit less shy and more easy socially, he suddenly seemed to leap streets ahead in the confidence stakes. I know it was hard for him, but he'd done it. Hard for me, though, to judge just what I was getting myself into.

I really liked Declan, was moved by him even, by his innocence and his lack of expectation beyond certain very simple dreams. But I was afraid he needed something from me that I was not able to give him. I think, I know, he wanted a girlfriend of his very own, a sweetheart. And I wasn't that.

But how to let him down gently? I decided to field the question, sidestep it.

'Why not come and see a play one night and we'll go for a drink?'

'All right so.' He seemed to accept that as an alternative.

'Come on Thursday if you can. It's *The Country Boy*, I think you'll like that.'

We went back with the others.

'All right so.' Declan shone. He looked round the faces. 'This has been the best day of my life.'

'Aah,' said Kitty and hugged him.

So did I.

Battersea, Summer 1947

I know a lot of people at school now. It's funny, my two best girlfriends are in the Blues and I'm in the Yellows, but we're still friends. Every time there's a test, if you come top it's more points for your team. I quite often do, and so does Rita. She's a Blue. Rita Bepay Westley Tarapor. Another person who comes top is Lance Secretan. He's sometimes quite naughty but I like him because he's got shining yellow-white hair and very smiling eyes. I'm sad because I think he's going to a boarding-school quite soon and I'll miss him. Sometimes he's my partner on the walk. Or I may get Leon da Brunna or Yurek Shrybeck. I really love Yurek most of all but he would rather be Carol's partner.

My other best friend apart from Rita is Judy Sharpe and she lives along the drive. I love going to her flat because she's got crowds of American friends who send her comics and we just read for hours and hours.

When I'm reading American comics I begin to feel what it would be like to live there and my voice changes and I say 'Hi' and 'cute' and I feel sad and excited at the same time because I want to go there and I might never make it. Judy may go on a holiday one day because her family has friends there. I wish I had.

Rita, my other friend, lives quite near school in a very special flat with folding doors, and we have to play quite quietly because their neighbours don't like a lot of noise. Rita's 'a real beauty' says Mama.

'Am I a beauty, Mama?'

'You've got a very interesting face.'

One problem.

When I take the short cut through the alley, children from round the back pull my beret off and say I'm posh. I'm not. It's funny because in school some people say I speak wrong, because I say 'bath' and 'glass' and not 'barth' and 'glarss'. Oh well.

I'm not going the long way round though.

Christmas 1947

They don't have a May Queen here, thank goodness, because I don't think they would choose me here either. Anyway, I didn't get chosen to be Our Lady in the Nativity Play. I think you have to have blonde hair. Mary Wheeler was Mary, and I was only an angel. It's terrible being an angel because you can't say anything, just fly on and look holy and you can't be sad or afraid or joyful, just solidly holy. Gabrielle Stoddard was an angel too and she has very blonde hair and a very shining, beautiful face. I think she looks like Our Lady. Mary Wheeler's just good and quiet. Roger Castillo was a shepherd and trod on my frock. I like him though.

Christmas was wonderful. Everyone came down here for the holidays, Auntie, Grandad, Frank. Hilda went back to Liverpool to be with Grandma and Grandad Collins and

George and Eric. George is going to be a Jesuit but not for a long while.

Mama moved everything round a bit to fit everyone in, and I was a bit worried in case Father Christmas wouldn't know where to find us. I left a note for him to say we'd be in the playroom, and be careful of the fire, but there was a change at the last minute, and Gabe and I were in where Maurice had been. Mama said he always knows where you are, just think and he knows.

I love waking up to that feeling like a dog on your feet – I miss Terry, poor Terry – and you don't know what it is because everything's wrapped up.

I got all the things which I like. The best presents from Father Christmas were a Red Indian outfit and a sleeping doll with a yellow suit, handknitted by Mother Christmas. And Mama and Dada gave me a real grown-up desk with three drawers for keeping things in. I also had a big pile of books and annuals. I love that. The best this year was Cynthia Asquith's Annual *from Auntie and* Little Gold Boy *from Maurice. It's lovely going right down to the last bit of the stocking. You know there's going to be an apple and an orange, and a new penny; but sometimes there's a funny surprise like, this year, a little falling-down spotted dog that springs out of shape when you press the bottom.

I went along to Judy's to show her my doll and she had a sleeping doll too, only hers had hair and looked sort of American, with American clothes. I expect Father Christmas knows she might go there one day.

We all went to eleven-o'clock Mass and lit candles round the crib. All the Castigliones were there and Roland and Gabe and I walked back together, and he said we could play cricket with him when summer comes. Roland's in my class, and they live in the drive too. Roland and his parents in one block and old M. and Mme Castiglione in another with the rest of the family.

Dada's going to help Roly a bit with his work and Mrs Castiglione said if I would like to go to her place for tea on

Fridays, I can learn French with Roly. I don't know anything about French.

I love French. I think I want to go there when I'm grown up.
   Every Friday, straight from school, Roly and I go to his Grandma's for 'le goûter'. That's tea. And we have 'du pain' and 'de la confiture'.
   Then when we've eaten, we read Jeannot Lapin *and play pic-a-stix in French, or cards. It's easy with Mme Castiglione because she just speaks to us and suddenly we understand. When I speak French I feel different. I feel neat and shruggy and my mouth is like a kiss.*

That night after the show I went with Tony and Vincent and Maggie to the dance at the Cahernane. It was a relaxed end to a day of treading gently and worrying about Declan's feelings.

Tony was on great form. His hair was brushed back revealing his fine forehead. Every now and then he would rake it back into place with those beautiful hands; narrow, delicate fingers, guitar fingers. He played a bit. I liked his hair that way. It showed him clear-eyed, witty. Sometimes when he brushed it over to one side he could look completely different. Sombre, grouchy. Sometimes I thought he had two faces, one sunny and funny, the other closed and difficult. I don't know whether the hair made the mood or the mood made the hair.

Not that he was often out of sorts, just that it was noticeable. Often the change coincided with a bad asthma attack which left him strained and tired.

But that night he was the best company in the world. We all danced with each other in twos, threes and fours. I danced a lot with Tony which I hadn't done before. I found it surprisingly easy. He moved me in the right

73

direction with a light touch and helped me be less self-conscious. I felt good next to him. I liked the smell of him.

When we got back to town he walked me down to New Street.

'Maybe they're all still up. Come and have a cup of tea.'

We pushed open the door and went through to the kitchen. The light was on but everything was cleared except a plate of bread and cheese left out for me. There was a big pot of tea too, hugged in a cosy with a towel thrown over it for extra warmth. It was still really fresh and hot. We shared a cup and made sandwiches, chatting softly so's not to disturb Cis away in her nest in the back.

'How was the picnic, with the dotey Declan? You haven't really told me.'

'It was fine. You'd have enjoyed it,' said I guiltily.

'You didn't ask me.'

'I know.'

'Why?'

'I don't know, I suppose . . .'

'Did you think I'd spoil it for you?'

'No, I . . . I thought it might spoil it for him.'

'Jealous.'

'No, no. Not jealous – unnerved – no reason to be jealous anyway.'

'No.'

'I mean, he's just a friend, a kind of lonely thing. Jealousy doesn't come into it.'

'For you. Maybe it does for him.'

'I know – maybe. Anyway you weren't there, smart arse, so he had absolutely nothing to be jealous about.'

We laughed – too loud – and shushed ourselves and laughed even louder! I pushed him out into the hall.

'Go on. Get out. Good night.'

'I'm going.'

I held open the door for him.

'It was a lovely evening, thanks.'

We stood smiling at each other in the kindly street lamps of New Street.

'It was great, good night.' And without taking his hands from his pockets, Tony leaned forward and kissed me on the cheek. I closed the door and wished it were more.

On Thursday *The Country Boy* played like a dream. We had a great house, lots of Americans and their response, as ever, was generous and immediate. Thunderous clapping, bags of tears and standers at the end.

I was surprised when I came out of the theatre to see not only Declan, standing nervously in the shadows, but also Dan and Eamonn. They steamed forward.

'It was great. You were great. You're a real actress.'

'Thanks.' I was pleased. I think I'd gone up in their estimation – more than a friendly grope on the 18th hole. I was someone to be a bit proud of.

I was conscious of Declan dying a thousand quiet deaths in the background, and brought him into the group. He handed me a box of Terry's All Gold.

'These are for you.'

'Aah, Declan, you shouldn't.'

'Yarrah now, you're a real stage-door Johnny,' hooted Eamonn. Declan looked at his shoes.

So here I was with three fellers, all ready for a drink.

'Will we go to the Grand?' said Dan.

'What about O'Leary's?' I said, desperate to get among the Company and lighten the load.

'Ah no,' said Eamonn. 'We'll be stuffed in the snug. No ladies in the bar.'

'OK, the Grand.'

Just then Tony and Maggie came out.

'Come for a drink,' I begged. 'Come to the Grand.'

'We're going to O'Leary's.'

'Just one in the Grand.' Tony must have seen the mute appeal in me.

'OK.'

We made a big table as Dan got a round in. Declan had hardly spoken.

'Did you like the play, Dec?'

'It was beautiful, but very sad. It made me realize that I—'

'There you are, Declan, Powers and water.'

'Thanks.' Declan turned back to me. 'I . . .'

Eamonn came and sat on the arm of my chair. 'Jaze, you were great. I loved the song.'

'When are we going to see Maggie, and you, Tony?'

'Saturday. Come on Saturday.'

'Tony sings too, then. Brings the house down.'

Tony moved to the bar. 'What'll you all have?'

Declan downed his whiskey. 'I wouldn't have minded going to America.'

'Well off you go, Dec,' Dan laughed.

'I can't. I have responsibilities.'

'What?'

'Mammy can't do without me.'

'Aah, you've got to look after yourself, Declan. Take care of Number One.'

'Well, I was . . .'

'Will we go to the Europa? Make a night of it?' Eamonn was ready for action.

'Yeah,' said Maggie. 'I like it there.'

'No, I won't,' said I. Suddenly I wanted away from it all. I didn't want to end up on the 18th hole or to be walking Killarney's streets with poor Declan.

'Oh, come on,' Dan put his arm round me.

'No, I'm sorry, I really can't. Tony and I have to go over the second scene of *Drama at Innish*. There's a change. We promised Jim.'

'What change?' Tony, blank, letting me down.

'You know, just before the doctor comes in. The new lines.' I threw him a desperate psychic wink.

'Oh, the new lines. God, yes, I forgot. Jim'll kill us.'

Everybody stood up and started to move out. Eamonn opened his car door for Maggie and Dan got in behind. He leaned out of the window as the car started up.

'Do you want to come, Deco?'

'No, no thanks.' He turned to face me.

'Thanks again for the chocolates, Declan. I'm sorry I have to go so soon.'

'That's all right. Good night so. Good night, Tony.'

'Good luck, Declan.'

'Will I see you at the dance?'

'Yes, of course. I'll be there. Good night.'

We walked away towards New Street, Tony and I. I turned back to see Declan waving a familiar red hand in salute.

'Good night.'

I felt sad and ashamed but I found I actually really wanted to be with Tony.

Back at New Street everybody moved up when we walked into the kitchen. Cis was still about.

'Don't stand on ceremony, Tony, make yourself at home.' Then she brought him a plate and a cup. From that night on, there was always a place for Tony at supper in New Street.

Summer 1948

I'm worried about the poor sewer rat in the fairground. There's a little zoo and you have to pay 1d to go in. I go to see him every day and take him bits of food. When I first went, he was just sitting in the corner looking hopeless. Nobody looks at him much because he's not fluffy or sweet. He's quite big and dirty. I don't think they wash him. I think he knows me now. His face brightens up when I bang on the cage and say: 'Hello, boy.'

But I'm worried when I go back to London at the end of the summer, he'll be on his own again.

Mrs Iv. makes beautiful cheese scones. She brought some down from upstairs and also something very strange and lovely – dried bananas. Mama says she's nearly a vegetarian but not all the children are. There's four of them and we play with John quite a lot. He's a bit older than me.

Once when he was locked out, Gabe and I rolled him up to the little balcony on the rubbish lift. He was very heavy and it's a long way up.

Mrs Iv. gets very fed up and tired going right up to the top. Sometimes she rattles on our door for a cup of tea.

One day when Mama opened it, she was very puffed. She just stood there.

'Forty years of effing shopping.'
Now then!

Winter 1948

Something wonderful happened. A sixth-form girl who was playing the 'Child' in The Dear Departed *dropped out of Mama's drama group because she had to study for her exams, and Mama asked me to do it. I quickly learned the lines and Mama rehearsed me at home and then I had to go at night to the drama group and do it with the real people. The first time I did it then my stomach was churning, but I felt quite good because everyone looked pleased and relieved.*

Then came the First Night. I was really very frightened because I knew a lot of people would be watching in the audience, including Dada and Maurice and Gabe.

There's a bit before I come on, when they go off and I have to do a sort of run on and bit of a look and call for 'Grandad', and I have to do a Lancashire accent.

Just before I went on, my heart was thumping and Mama told me 'Now' and I took a deep breath and ran on.

The stage felt much different than in the rehearsals. It was all bright and felt like a real front-room even though all the audience was there. Mama said: 'Don't look at the audience. You can look out thinking, but not straight at them.'

I didn't know what she meant before but now I do.

When I looked out thinking, Where's me Grandad? I made them into the back of my mind so they could know I was thinking, Where's me Grandad? and I could feel all of them breathing and I wasn't afraid any more and when I said: 'Where's me Grandad?' everyone laughed and it was wonderful, and later on when I said: 'Eee, Grandad, I am glad you're not dead,' everyone laughed and clapped. And I didn't want to come off.

I'm not sure how it suddenly came about because I don't remember discussing it, but the next afternoon, instead of taking the demesne trail or aiming for the lakeshore we walked, Tony and I, towards the back of the town and out to the new estate and Tony's digs.

And there in his quiet plain room in the silent little house, we made love for the very first time.

I couldn't have wished for a sweeter first lover. Tony had a rare delicacy and gentleness that made my rite of passage very easy. No sweat, no strain, no angst. We were lifted on the same soft wind to infinity.

That day began for me a period of unique happiness. I loved being one of a pair. I loved the way our humour coincided exactly, and that when some minute incident struck us as funny, Tony had only to let the merest downturn of mouth or lift of brow flit across his face to register our mutual collapse.

I loved being on the stage with him. Every pleasure was heightened because I had someone to share it with.

We did everything together. Pat used to call us the Bisto Kids. It was happening for her and Liam too. Sometimes in New Street we'd hug each other, Liam and I, scarcely believing our luck.

I know it sounds mawkish and very unfeminist but I just loved belonging to him. Being his girl. Aah, but I was young then!

Because it was rooted in friendship, it was a good kind of love, Tony's and mine; not a love that excluded others, rather one that was a part of the group, not isolated from it. We continued to do lots of things with the others, often Pat and Liam, but often in the afternoon we'd bike out to Castle Island, to the lakeshore and make love in a place almost untouched by time. Sometimes we talked – sometimes we just took books and read. Although we were spending so much time with each other there seemed to be a perfect balance. We gave and received, it seemed, just the right amount of intensity to each other. I was extremely happy.

Towards the beginning of August, Pat and Jim gave us two surprises, one lovely, one not so lovely. The lovely was an extra ten bob a week which was wonderful and generous of them. They said the season was a really good one and I'd worked very hard, so deserved it. Good people.

The second surprise was another play. Everyone was gobsmacked. Another play this late in the season. It was *The Singer* by Padraig Pearce, a very good play if somewhat melodramatic. But a bit heavy and with a very difficult part for me. It was set in the 'wesht' of Ireland and I was to play Shelagh, a girl possessed by the devil – or so they thought.

I wasn't really experienced enough for that kind of stuff and I found the rehearsals very difficult. I became more and more disenchanted with myself and Jim, quite rightly, drove me very hard. One day I'd had enough and threw my first (and only) wobbler. It was a bit where I had to smash a statue of Our Lady and Jim felt I was not abandoning myself sufficiently to the moment. I flew into a rage.

'Right,' said I. 'Fini. I'm off.' And I flung the statue to

the floor. Exit weeping and cursing. Me, not the character. Jim and I raged at each other for a good three minutes and then he suddenly gave me a hug.

'And you know what?' he said. 'That's exactly the way to do it,' and laughed. And so did I, and I went back and got on with it.

The Singer was a moderate success. I acquitted myself adequately – and do you know what the best bit was? When I threw the statue. I smashed it to smithereens every night and the audience loved it, especially when bits flew into their midst and they kept them as souvenirs.

Summer 1949

We've arrived. Home again. Auntie opened the door and said: 'You're here.' And we all kissed each other.

'Scamp was here this morning waiting for you. That dog never comes near the place then she just knows when you're coming.'

Gabe and I went straight outside and did our special whistle and then down from the top of the drive she came. Scamp. Spanielly face, beautiful black-and-white spots. Collie tail and bottom all wagging at once. She licked us all over. Way up at the top of the drive Scamp's lady waved to us. She lets Scamp be our dog all through the summer.

I saw Mrs Morrison on the way back in and gave her a wave. They live downstairs. Then we got all our buckets and spades out from the gas cupboard under the stairs. I found a small dead crab in one of my buckets. It didn't look very nice.

I'm sleeping in the box-room this year. Gabe'll stay in with Mama and Auntie till Dada and Maurice come, then there'll be a change round. I love the box-room. It's tucked away and quiet if you haven't got to share it with anyone.

Last year I was in with Grandad in his room. That was

81

good too because his bedroom's next to Jean Anderson's and we sent each other letters on a string pulley. We'll go and see the Andersons after tea.

Phil and Marg are here now. And they're allowed to stay a couple of days. I love it when they stay because the four of us do different things. Sometimes we gang up on each other – Phil and Gabe against me and Marg.

When the tide's very far out, we go all across the rocks and on to the sandbank for our picnic. It's wonderful on the far side of the sandbank. When you're first there it's completely smooth, like the moon or a magic land where no one's been. Sometimes when I first get there I don't want to speak. I just want to be there and be quiet.

You have to be careful though because when the tide turns, it comes in fast. You have to judge it. The way to know best is keep looking at the little stream between the sandbank and the rocks, and when it gets wider and faster and the pooees and rubbish start floating by, that's the time to leave, because the sewage pipe is opened and the tide's coming in.

Once we nearly left it too late and it was hard to wade through the stream. It came nearly up to our waists and past Marg's and big pooees kept floating by and hitting us. Horrible.

We're all making butter today. We've got jam jars with milk in, screwed tight, and you tie them round your waist and keep them there all day and all the bobbing up and down and running and jumping makes the milk into butter.

I nearly smashed my jam jar. We were playing in the bomb damage, next to our house and Pat Hurley dared me to jump across the broken floorboards over the cellar. It's a huge drop. I half fell, only just made it and bashed my arm and leg on the girder! I won't tell Mama though.

The Andersons have got a whole house so Jenny Anderson's let us have their box-room as a playroom for wet days. We've done it up beautifully. We've got loads of books and a trunk from Mama to keep things in and for an extra seat.

There're two stools and a deckchair and a tea set.

Our best thing at the moment is pontoon. We play for matchsticks. If it was money, Gabe would be rich! She's the best.

We've got a kettle too but we can only use that if Jenny lights the fire, and it's not worth it unless it's really cold and a bad day's well set in.

We call it the Attic Club and I wrote a little song for us:

> *On the good ship Rub a Dub*
> *It's a nice trip to the Attic Club.*
> *Where four girls play*
> *On a rainy or a miserable day.*

We've found a really good place to go. If there's no band in Vale Park or if we're fed up with the fairground, we go the other way, past the frightening drives Elgin and Caithness till we get to a lovely café and they do beautiful teas.

Even if Jean doesn't go we always take Catherine in the pushchair. The first time we went, I was a bit shocked at the prices because we have to make our pocket money last right through the holiday. But the man in charge said, Don't worry, pay what we could. I think he likes us. Maybe feels a bit sorry for us. Catherine can look a bit tragic sometimes, like a poor child. You just say, 'Look sad, Cath,' and she just does it.

Anyway we have beautiful cream teas now for next to nothing and the man is really kind to us. He even showed us round the back where the kitchen is. Once when he was standing by me I might have seen his trouser buttons all undone, but I don't think I did.

One bright day towards the end of August a whirlwind blew into Killarney. She arrived on the E.S.B. lorry some time towards noon, with just herself and a bit of an old carpet-bag of possessions, and swept us off our feet.

Eileen Murphy.

I remember Jim introducing her with a look of great affection, admiration, exasperation.

'This is the Murf, last year's juve and the year before. Star of stage, screen and Telefis Eireann.'

She had the blackest hair, the bluest eyes, the whitest skin and the most energy of anyone I'd ever met. It's funny isn't it, the first moment you meet someone who's going to be your friend for life. You don't know that. I simply saw someone I was immediately both drawn to and intimidated by. I was envious of her terrific confidence, her great style. She had an ability to create something unique out of the most unpromising raw material. Dress. Rooms. Situations.

Much later on in our lives I went to visit her in one of the hundreds of homes she's had and in the midst of bare walls, tea-chests and cold winter floorboards, she gave me tea in a china cup from a silver pot, with a single rose in the middle of the tray.

She never has, never had, any money but somehow she makes her patch special.

'How are ye, Chrissie?' she said, dumping her bag beside me. Why was I Chrissie? Everyone's Chrissie in Dublin.

'I'm great. What are you having?'

'I'll have a half. So – are ye all going to the dance tonight?' And the ice is broken and we talk like old friends, all of us.

Tony loved her and especially wanted to know about the lie of the land in Telefis. Murf promised to tote us round in Dublin to meet a few people. And said we could stay with her. She was riding high at that time. She'd just finished a hugely successful series and was about to start on another one.

She walked down to New Street at lunch-time to see if Sally and Cis would give her a little corner for the few days she'd be there.

'They're full. But you can kip in with me if you don't mind a double bed.'

'Aah, Chrissie, you're a little dote. Thanks.'

Cis greeted her with open arms and Sal made another place at the table. The Gardaí got big French kisses and blushed and John McMahon tried hard to hide his love of her with squints and mutterings till she broke down his defences.

'Give us an old kiss, John.'

'Oh God, let me look at the child. What in the name of God are you wearing?'

Black, lots of black, and huge amounts of eye make-up. Short skirt, fishnet tights. I felt very safe and colourless beside her.

After the show that night a huge gang of us went to the dance and Eileen was the belle of the ball. She was a terrific dancer, wild and free, and it wasn't until much later that I noticed she had a limp – polio in childhood has left her with a shorter leg. But she never let it hold her back one iota.

She even knew the band! She knew everybody. And those she didn't, she soon did. She's a great communicator, she's brave at making the first move. I tried to learn that from her.

For the first time that night I found myself feeling insecure about Tony. For no good reason. But he and Murf danced a lot together and well. They had an immediate rapport. There was in them both more than a little of the free spirit, an ability to change course in mid direction. I felt they were both 'one bag' people. I wondered to myself if he found me smothering, too earthbound.

Nevertheless it was a good night and on the way home, as we passed the theatre, Tony held me back behind the others with a butterfly touch on the shoulder.

'Here.' He pulled me through the entrance pillars and away into a little soft corner by the prop store, and loved me just when I needed it.

They've cut my hiding-hole down. I went there with my lunch and my book and it was just gone. All the long thick reedy grasses, all gone.

There was a bulldozer there and piles of rubbish and stones and bits of railing. There were a couple of workmen standing around and I went over to them.

'What's happening? Why is this all cut down?'

'Festival of Britain, mate.'

'Well, so what?'

'Gonna be a funfair here, love. Smashing, eh?'

'I've had a funfair. I want my hiding-hole back.'

'Too late, mate. Sorry, love.'

I was in a bit of a rage so I hurried away back to my holly tree by the lake. That's our bit of the park. A girl was standing near it looking interested so I glared very hard at her and made a few chimpanzee noises. That frightened her away. I tied my picnic bag to the rope and climbed up to the top seat part. Then I pulled up my lunch and book.

It's peaceful in that tree. You can read for hours and watch people through the leaves and they don't know you're here. You can see the boats on the lake too. Gabe's got the tree next door which is a bit taller but mine's more cosy and round.

I mean, I loved my hiding-place but really this is better, so thank God I've got one thing left.

I wonder what it'll be like having a funfair here – it won't be anything like New Brighton.

August 1950

Molyneux Road, Liverpool.

It's very peaceful staying with Grandma and Hilda. I always feel a bit old-fashioned here. The house sounds are all old-fashioned. The clock in the kitchen chimes every quarter of an hour, the same as the Morrisons', but it's much tingier.

And when I do my piano practice in the parlour, the piano sounds very thin and plinky-plonky. I think it's quite old because the keys are yellow, much smaller than our Bechstein and the candle-holders are still on it. I love the parlour. It's very small and quiet with antimacassars on all the chairs and lace curtains on the window, all very white and clean.

We're mostly in the kitchen though, the sitting kitchen. Grandma cooks and does the washing in the back kitchen. Sometimes I do a bit of mangling for her but I'm a bit nervous since I caught my fingers in the rollers. It's much bigger than ours, and very heavy.

We're having soused herrings for tea. That's my favourite. Nobody else makes them. I'm laying the table. You have to take off the chenille cloth and put a white one over the oilcloth.

It's my birthday soon and so we're having a cake tonight in honour of it. I know as well there's something for me in the cards on the mantelpiece. It's always the same and I love it. Two cards, one from Grandma and one from Hilda. And when I open them something will fall out. A pound note from Grandma's and a ten-bob note from Hilda's – they're always crisp and new – lovely.

Autumn 1950

Miss Packer's never really liked me. I don't know why. I work very hard and I don't play around in class, but sometimes she has a look as if she despises me. I used to try to make her like me but I don't any more. She's not wonderful to anyone but she has a couple of favourites.

I'm always first or second so it's not the work. Once I was talking, not much, so was Carol, but she made me stand outside the classroom. And Sister Teresa Joseph came by and said: 'What on earth are you doing there? You're always a very good girl.'

Maybe it's because I'm a teacher's child. Mama says some

people don't like teachers' children because you can't fool them.

Or maybe she's cross because I was in a play at Mama's school. I sang 'Greensleeves' in the pageant. They needed someone to look young. All the people at Mama's school are grown-up. They were marvellous. Frances Dix sang like a nightingale; Dada said she should be a professional and 'Queen Elizabeth' was like a real queen. Mama says nobody cares about them though. No one will help them because they're the bottom of the Secondary Mod. Everyone used to say they were useless but Mama proved they're not. In the pageant they're wonderful.

When I stopped worrying about Miss Packer not liking me was when I did The Little Matchgirl. *I made a whole play, wrote it, acted the Little Matchgirl and produced everybody else in it. I did it for the whole school, and everyone was really enjoying it. They loved it when I saw visions of my grandma in the flame. But every time I fainted from hunger, and when I was dying at the end, I had to lie down, and every time I did, Miss Packer shouted from the back in a loud voice: 'Can't see you.'*

'Can't see you. Stand up.'

How can you die standing up? I was really fed up.

I'll still give her a present at the end of term. But now I don't care if she likes it or not.

I was really devastated a week later when Sally called me in to the back kitchen and said I'd have to vacate my room for the teacher. I couldn't believe it.

'But where can I go?'

'Don't worry about it. Kitty has two beds in her room, and she'll be delighted to have you.'

Poor Kitty! I don't think she had much choice. She was on some kind of rock-bottom permanent resident deal that included sharing her room whenever necessary.

Over the next few days I slowly cleared out my lovely room. How would I bear it not looking out over the night-lit New Street? Kitty's room was smaller, looked on to the yard and was overflowing with her lifelitter. She was genuinely delighted to have my company and grew quite tearful when I assured her it was only three more weeks.

Only three weeks. And then what? Stay in Dublin? I didn't want to leave Ireland. I felt at home there. This was a good place for me. I started to cry too.

'Oh, Kitty.'

'Oh, darlin'. Here, have a little snifter to cheer you up.'

She pulled up the bedspread and reached under her bed. 'Here.' She held out a bottle of Sanatogen Tonic Wine, nearly empty.

'Kitty?'

'Ah, go on, help yourself.' She gave a little kick under the bed with her slipper. 'I've another one below.'

'Aah, Kitty.'

The new teacher was not made dreadfully welcome by us, poor thing. She was quite solemn and found us too self-centred and established, I'm sure. I couldn't even begin to see her good points. To me all she represented was a broad presence barring me for ever from the top floor of New Street.

As we moved into our final week, everyone was talking about their plans for the winter.

Cecil had no problems. He was a summer actor. Winter would be spent as ever in the warmth of the bakery. I liked the way Cecil divided his life. He loved acting but not enough to schlep round cold halls in the winter months.

Joan was going home to Dublin. She saved and planned well and would wait for something good to come up. Maybe do a bit of private nursing.

Both Pat and Jim were established enough to return to Dublin, knowing they'd get some television or theatre work.

Vincent had loads of options. He was an enthusiastic

jack of all trades, and would act, stage-manage, adminis-
trate, do a tele, go on the dole – whatever.

I was worried about Noel and John. They'd written
crowds of letters, hoping for one of the better tours, but
so far the only definite offer was from Paddy Feeney's
Travelling Circus.

'But what on earth are you going to do in that?' I asked
John, one breakfast-time.

'Oh, sketches. Two comedy, one melodrama. Between
the acts.' He crossed his eyes at me and turned his head
away. 'Not grand enough for you, no doubt. Twenty-five
pounds and a touring allowance.'

'No, it sounds great, John. I just haven't seen anything
like that in England.' I knew he hated it, so I stopped
talking and gave us all more tea instead.

Liam was certainly going to stay with Pat for a while
but he had quite a good career in Canada and was
thinking of giving it another go.

Tony had already had a chat with one of the E.S.B.
fellows and was sorting out a lift to Dublin. He asked me
how soon I'd be ready. We were all leaving each other. I
couldn't bear it.

Suddenly one night on the way to the theatre, just
Liam and I, he turned to me.

'I don't want to go.'

'What?'

'I don't want to leave just yet. I want a bit of time on
my own. Will ye stay?'

'Yes.' I knew exactly what he meant. I felt just the
same. It wasn't that we didn't love our lovers, just that
we suddenly had a desperate need to stop giving and
taking for five minutes. To tune in to nothing but the
town and the stopping and ourselves.

It would be easier to do it together. To plead a week's
rest. A few days to 'do' the beauty spots. Pat and Tony
wouldn't mind. We'd be together but we wouldn't ask
anything of each other.

Tony and Pat didn't mind a bit. Maybe we fancied ourselves too much. Maybe they'd be glad of the break too.

The end came before we knew it.

On Saturday we were a family. On Sunday everyone was gone. Tony went on the train with the rest of the Dublin contingent, and to hell with the expense.

John and Noel were leaving at three o'clock from the roundabout at the edge of town. Paddy Feeney's lorry would be by to pick them up.

Cis had packed them sandwiches and tea, and Johnny, the Town Hall caretaker, had a barrow borrowed from the station, and would push their trunks to the meeting point. Liam and I went to see them off.

I felt as though we were of another age as we walked through the street. John strode in his cloak-coat. Noel sauntered along behind, ciggy in hand, coughing a bit in the September morning. And Johnny pushed the barrow down the middle of the road like some Dickensian pallbearer.

'Goodbye, John.' A wave.

'Good luck, Noel.'

There stands Con, arms folded in the doorway.

'You're not getting off without a kiss, John.' Kitty running from Hilliards, stuck with pins and tape measure round her neck.

'Ooh God, woman.' A brief peck.

At the roundabout (Cork exit) we waited. Three o'clock. Ten past. Twenty-five past. Noel sat on his trunk and lit up again. John looked down the road – and beyond.

'Don't wait any more.'

'We don't mind.'

'Don't wait.' He didn't want us to be there.

'OK. Goodbye, John. You've been – I love you, John.' A quick hug.

'Bye, Noel, love ya. Good luck.'

Liam and I turned towards town. We looked back –
once. There they were – two old men sitting on their
trunks waiting for the circus to take them away.

*I'm having a marvellous time. Mama says it's time stolen
out of eternity – when you should be at school and you're
not.*

*Two things made it happen. First of all Miss Packer said
I couldn't take the scholarship. I'm in my third year in the top
class but she won't let me take it because I'm too young. She
says I'll do better next year. Maybe I will but I just keep
doing the work over and over again. Anyway that was one
reason I'm here.*

*The second thing was very sad. Grandad died. We knew
he was going to die because he had the cancer, all over him,
and it kept hurting him. All through the summer I knew it
was hurting him very much when he whistled and sang with
his teeth clenched.*

> *Sing it again.*
> *The grand refrain*
> *When Gabriel sounds his last rally.*

But he never said.

I cried when Dada said Grandad had died.

*Anyway Auntie came down for Christmas and we all tried
to be happy because Grandad had certainly gone to Heaven
but it was hard.*

*Something else happened. I feel very silly now I know, but
it couldn't be helped and I've got over it now.*

*Just before Mama went home in the weeks Grandad was
dying, I was writing to Father Christmas and Mama
was watching me. I'd put a few things down – books – new
pen – party shoes – and then I was writing the main present –*

a Vulcan sewing-machine. I'd seen them in the shops – toy ones but they really worked.

She came over to the gate-leg table where I was sitting and looked over my shoulder.

'A sewing-machine? Are you sure you want that, Paul?'

'Yes, they're beautiful, you can make real things.'

'Wouldn't you like a lovely blue crêpe de Chine frock?'

'No, I really want a Vulcan sewing-machine.'

'Father Christmas might not be able to manage that. It's very dear.'

'He can, Mum. He can give you anything so long as you're not greedy.'

'But he's got a lot of people to cater for.'

'Well, I've said he needn't bother about anything else much. Just that.'

Then she burst into tears. Mama cried and cried and said: 'There's no Father Christmas. It's me and your Dada, and we can't afford it. We just haven't got the money for a Vulcan sewing-machine. I'm sorry, lovie. I'm sorry.'

Then we both cried and Gabe came in and said I was stupid. She knew years ago there was no Father Christmas. Then I felt a fool.

It's funny now that I look back. How on earth did I go on believing in him, even when Carol Smith and Yurek said I was an idiot?

Anyway a lot of things happened at the end of the year to make me feel more grown-up and now here I am.

I'm with Auntie in Wallasey for the whole of this term! I'm keeping her company now Grandad's gone. Mama said I'd done the work so many times I can afford to miss a term, and Dada's given me some IQ tests to practise, and I'll do some compositions.

We're having a lovely time, Auntie and I.

We have breakfast together before she goes to school, then I potter around or go to Jenny Anderson's, next door, for my dinner. Some days I go to collect Catherine from school for Jenny and take her down to the shore in the afternoon but it's really too cold for that.

Some days I go to Auntie's school with her, and help with the little ones. Or sometimes she puts me on the bus at the Pierhead in Liverpool and I go to visit Grandma in Molyneux Road or Auntie Cissie, in Fazakerley.

I love going on the ferry from Seacombe to the Pierhead. When you go down the long tunnel to the boat, there's a lovely spanking echo. I often dream about that tunnel. Sometimes in my dream I don't reach the boats. I get sidetracked down little winding staircases that lead to foreign lands, like China or France. Then I get lost in the strange places, but I'm really enjoying it. Sometimes I get to the end of the tunnel and the water isn't there. It's a railway track and a train instead. I love the ferry.

The best part of being with Auntie is the nights out. We go three or four times a week with Auntie's friend Hilda to the pictures or a show; or maybe on a Saturday to George Henry Lees in Liverpool and then Reeces for tea.

One of the nights out was a bit horrible though. We were going to see Madame Butterfly at the Royal Court in Liverpool, and I was really looking forward to it. I love 'One Fine Day'. I'm learning it and Auntie plays for me.

All through the show I kept waiting for Madame Butterfly but there was only a huge lady and then Auntie said: 'That's Madame Butterfly.'

And I said, 'She can't be. Butterfly's really little. It says "Little baby wife of mine".'

And then, it came to 'One Fine Day' and the huge lady sang it and when she sang 'Little baby wife of mine', I couldn't help crying because it wasn't really Butterfly.

Last Tuesday we went to see The Dancing Years at the Winter Gardens, just the two of us. Felt a bit guilty leaving Hilda out. It's a different place in the winter, Wallasey. The prom's empty and lonely and the waves are huge.

One day when it was a bit sunny I took Catherine to the

café where we used to go for our teas but it was all closed up.
I felt sad.

Liam and I spent ten days more in Killarney. We walked
the demesne, took a jaunting car round the Ring of Kerry
and took an extraordinary pleasure in being out in town
at night when things were still humming, having been in
the theatre every night for five months. It's a very odd
feeling being released. It takes some adjusting to. And
around nine o'clock every night, we started to feel guilty
as if there was something left undone.

We spent quiet times with Con in O'Leary's, talking of
our plans, and what we all wanted out of life. Much the
same, it seemed. Something ephemeral. Something not
very much to do with money or success. Something to do
with that completeness, oneness we all felt when we
stood by the lakeshore and became part of the great
silence. But what?

We actually didn't spend much time apart, Liam and
I. Because we were so undemanding of each other, we
never 'intruded on each other's personality'. Liam taught
me that phrase. He got it from a man in the street who
asked the way.

'Excuse me for intruding on your personality, but can
ye tell where the Post Office is?' Lovely.

On Sunday Liam said, 'Shall we go to one last
dance?'

'Yes, and shall we take Kitty?'

'Yes.'

We took a taxi seeing the occasion that was in it and
the fact that it was a chilly night. It was out the Muckross
Road, just like the first one. Not my favourite hall. The
band was doing its best but fighting a losing battle. It was
one of those segregated nights. For no good reason some
nights the hall would split in two, girls up one end near
the band, men umbilically tied to the bar. Murf would
have got them all going.

The singer was irretrievably flat and his echoing 'Shadow of Your Smile' a brave but foolhardy choice. This only added to the air of gloom.

We decided the only thing to do was to get stotious and fool ourselves into a good time so Liam bought a bottle of champagne. Wild extravagance! And we made Black Velvet with Guinness, which was lovely. And the three of us danced everything together, Kitty hanging on to the champagne in case it got pinched.

I saw Declan suddenly at the very end of the bar. I hadn't seen him arrive. He was just all at once there, holding a half between his two red hands, warming them. He gave the old salute, but didn't come across.

'I'm just going to have a word with Declan. Say goodbye,' I said. 'Dance amongst yourselves.'

Kitty laughed and took a swig of the old shampoo.

I felt a bit conspicuous tap tapping across an empty piece of floor.

'How are ye, Deco?'

'I'm great. Yourself?'

'Fine.'

'I was afraid you'd gone, then someone said you were still in town, and Liam too.'

'Yes, we couldn't bear to leave.'

Declan held his glass tightly and looked into the froth. 'I can't bear you to leave.'

'Oh, Deco.' I didn't know what to say. I didn't want to patronize him or make light of him.

'It's all right. I know you're Tony's girl . . .'

'I'm not. I'm my girl . . .'

'Very well so but . . . for now you're Tony's girl and your view of life is very different from mine – more expansive, but I want to tell you, I wish I'd had more time with you . . . I wish I'd known you more.'

For the first time since I'd met him Declan looked directly at me, no shuffling, no head hanging, and I saw the intensity in his eyes. Here was a man, a young man, probably younger than me, who had shut out his dreams for some reason of duty or lack of self-esteem.

'Declan, you can do anything you want, be anything you want. You'll find a wonderful girl who's right for you. You sing that old song and they'll be beating the door down.' I felt like some trashy agony aunt. Declan let me off the hook.

'All right so.' He smiled. 'But there'll never be another picnic like that one. There's Liam now waiting to take you away. Goodbye, Pauline.'

'Good night, Declan.'

He raised his hand. 'Goodbye.'

Summer 1951

Jean and I and Gabe committed sacrilege in Longbottoms Church at the bottom of Radnor Drive.

It was the day of the Orange Marches and we'd followed them up and down the drives shouting: 'Dirty old King Billy,' after the drummers. We got fed up after a while because nobody paid any attention to us.

We played bad eggs for a bit, where everyone has a number and someone throws the ball in the air and shouts a number, and if it's yours, you have to catch it. If you miss you've got one bad egg. Three, and you're out. But it's no good with only three of us.

So we went down to Longbottoms to play hide-and-seek in the churchyard. It's very overgrown in there. The church is locked and nobody ever goes there. It's a Proddy church. Nobody goes. Jean says it's haunted and she dared her cousin Pat to stay the night but she wouldn't.

We played a bit but it was always quite easy to find people. Then I found a door hanging off like a shed door. We always thought it was a shed before, when it was locked. But it was a lav. Well, half a lav. It was the hole where the lavatory goes into the ground, and the chain and cistern. I gave the chain a pull and then I had to leap back because all the water came rushing out.

I shouted Jean and Gabe to come and pulled the chain again. It was funny having all that chain pulling and water, and nothing for it to go into.

Suddenly we all wanted to pee.

'Guard me,' said Jean, pulling down her knickers, and peed in the hole. Then Gabe did but missed and it went on the floor. Then me. Then we all pulled the chain together, and rushed out, laughing.

'That's a sacrilege,' said Jean, trying to look strict.

'What's that?' Gabe was frightened.

'Not in a Protestant church,' I said. 'That's not a sacrilege.'

'Yes, it is,' said Jean in a deep voice. 'You have to tell it in confession.'

We were in the middle of the path leading to the gate when Jean called suddenly: 'Quick, quick. Someone's coming. Run, run.'

And we ran screaming and laughing all the way home.

I never did tell it in confession though.

Two days later I was banging on the door of Eileen's flat in Dublin. It opened and there was Tony, delighted to see me and thrilled to bits with Dublin. I found suddenly I'd really missed him. I wanted the feel of his easy contact, the scent of him, the comfort of his familiarity.

Eileen had fixed us up with tickets for Beckett's *Happy Days* that evening, and we were meeting her later at Neary's Bar. I had a bath and started to hunt some clothes out. Tony sat on the bed and watched me pad to and fro in a towel. I felt quite new again in the relationship, fancied him all over again. He was half-dressed and graceful, lounging on the bed. I went to him and kissed the piece of chest that wasn't buttoned. From then on Beckett had no chance.

We made the best love ever during the first act of

Happy Days. It was loving and caring and special.

We made the second act.

Dublin was a wonderful whirl of pubs and bars and people. We seemed to meet a million. Directors, producers, fixers, all of whom might be able to use us; none of whom actually did. But we had a great time. I remember one night in Neary's or Groom's: we were a big group, having a drink before a party when Murf hissed: 'Put your glass in your bag.'

'What?'

'Do it, Chrissie, put your glass in your bag.'

'Why?'

'For fuck sake.'

'OK.'

When we got outside she told me it was for the party. I walked through the streets of Dublin with 'guilty' branded across my forehead. I felt like an axe-murderer.

At the end of the week we decided to go back to England, Tony and I. We loved Dublin but it was plain to see that there really wasn't enough work for the Irish actors let alone incomers like us.

We got the night boat and stood on the deck long after Dun Laoghaire had disappeared, loath to let it go.

Summer 1952

I can't believe it. This is the very last summer I will ever spend in Wallasey. I feel desperate.

And all because of the Morrisons. I don't quite understand the ins and outs of everything but the gist of it is that Dada was the real tenant of Radnor Drive although everyone lived in it together. Us and Auntie, Grandad, Maurice, Frank, everyone. With all the confusion of the war, when we moved to London, nobody thought of changing the names, and now the council says we have to leave, because we're in London too much and Auntie's not the real tenant.

99

At first we argued, because we are here all the holidays, but then the Council said they had proof that Dada was only there certain months – not enough. And that's when we found out about the Morrisons. Mr Morrison had kept a diary of every moment Dada was there, and he'd given it to the Borough Council.

How could anybody do that? How could anybody live underneath us, and you can hear their lovely chiming clock, and smile at you every day for years, and do something like that?

So all our lives are changing. Auntie's coming to live with us and Maurice, so she'll be a London teacher now. Everything's happening at once. We're packing up this house and George is being ordained into a full Jesuit at the end of the summer, and I'm going to grammar school, Convent of the Sacred Heart in Hammersmith. So I've got a lot to look forward to, but all the new things are spoilt by losing this house.

It's been the most wonderful of summers. There's so many things we've done and I feel so sad we'll never do them again.

We found a good way of earning dough this year – by accident. We were all making sandpies like we always do; crushing the brown, soft stones into powder for chocolate, and bashing up the marble rocks for nuts, and pounding the soft, white ones for icing sugar. We made lots of lovely shapes and decorated them with shells. And then just for the finishing touch, we wrote 'Pat's Pantry' in shells on the stone ledge.

We were just sitting having our lunch when a voice shouted: 'Hello, Pat's Pantry.'

And there was an old man looking down from the prom.

'That's lovely work, girls. Here's a threepenny bit for your till.' And he threw it down. We couldn't believe it.

'Thanks. Thanks a million.'

A bit later on someone else threw some pennies down and we suddenly realized we were on to a good thing.

We organized it a bit better and put the 'Pat's Pantry' facing towards the prom and I found an old cap of Grandad's to catch the money. We got more cake tins too, to give people a better show. Jean'll probably do it next year and I won't be here.

Gabe and I used to go and help Goosy Lil too, in the fairground. She's got the stall where you throw a ball in the goose's mouth and win a prize when it hits a number.

'Prize Every Time. Every Time A Winner.'

Most of the prizes are rotten. You only get a big toy once in a blue moon. But Gabe and I play for nothing and when there are trippers around, Lil gives us big prizes so everyone thinks it's easy and they all want to play. Then we go round the side and give them back. Sometimes Lily gives us money if it's a good day, but mostly it's just a small prize. I like being a stooge. I like Lil. I'll miss her.

Last weekend we all went over the water to stay with Grandma, and Frank did something fiendish. Most of the furniture's gone into store now and the carpets. So it's all bare boards. And just before we left, Frank put the radiogram on 'repeat play' with a record of 'Sailing Up The Clyde' because the Morrisons are Scotch and then he switched the hoover on, standing on the bare boards, and left them going for a night and a day. And the Morrisons didn't dare complain.

This afternoon I took the number one bus to Seacombe because soon I'll never go on it again; and I walked all the way back along the prom. I felt very sad and a bit lonely but I quite like that feeling. Past all the drives I don't know, past the dark bit of the prom that doesn't get much sun, past the frightening drives, Elgin and Caithness. Even them I'll miss. And then standing at the bottom of Radnor, looking at the river, suddenly the tide is full and high and dashing up over the railings all across the prom spraying me, wetting everything.

This is the neap tide.

This is the end of the summer.

Home Again

Once we were back Tony and I decided to have a little rest from each other while we made contact with our families and friends, and tried to sort out some new work. I re-registered with the L.C.C. as being available for supply work as a teacher, and started to see my friends.

Much as I had loved Killarney, it was wonderful to be back in London.

It was a beautiful late September and the trees along Prince of Wales Drive were very full. Sitting on the balcony the first night I was back, voices and footsteps felt very near as they always did through the summer. All through my childhood I'd loved sitting out on summer nights.

It was a very narrow balcony just one chair wide and about twelve feet long, big enough though, when Gabe and I were young, to pull our mattresses out and sleep in the open air on a hot night.

At that time I shared the flat with my sister Gabe and my friend, Marie McGaughey, whom I'd met at drama school.

In 1959 Mama and Dada and her two brothers and sisters had decided to pool their resources and get out of rented accommodation and London, by buying a house together.

They were seaside children, the Callanans, and Mama in particular had never really taken to smoky London and they eventually chose a house in Worthing, a couple of miles from the sea.

It had three living-rooms – good for this rare ménage – and four bedrooms. They converted the garage into a garden annexe for Frank who was only sporadically in England, and the bedrooms went to my parents, Uncle Maurice and Auntie Pauline, and my sister Claire, who was then six. It cost £6,000.

Our flat, once owned by the Council, had since passed to a private landlord and was five pounds a week. This was a huge burden for Dada on top of his mortgage, but he decided to keep it on until we finished our further education. Things drifted on and we still had it and I still didn't pay any rent.

Marie had come to the flat in our first year at drama school. She was the daughter of a professor of veterinary surgery at the University of Kandi in Ceylon, now Sri Lanka. From the moment we met we knew each other. We shared a bedroom for three years and never exchanged an angry moment.

She was a magnificent dancer, a great lover of people and parties. She was a loving and supportive friend then, and still is thirty odd years later. We have watched each other grow over those years. We have known and shared delight and sorrow, trauma and peace. But then we were young mates. All yet to come.

It was to this home then that I returned in September.

A couple of days later I went down to Worthing to see the family.

Mama met me at the station. Big hugs and kisses, then: 'Your skin's a bit spotty. And your hair's lost its shine – I thought Irish rain was meant to be wonderful for the skin.'

Does losing your virginity mean losing your shiny hair? I hoped not.

I spent a happy week or so in Worthing in idle sloth, except for the odd trot along the beach. I shopped a bit and cooked a bit for the returning workers, played big sister to Claire, occasionally defended her against the adult household, and wondered where my next job was coming from.

I was not particularly ambitious, a trait that was reflected in the fact that I had not yet made contact with my agent, James Sharkey, a handsome and charming young man at the huge Al Parker organization. I'd only met him once or twice. First when I'd been more or less forced on him by Barry Shawzin whom I'd met on my very first job, and later on for a kind of re-cap on each other. He'd sent me for some jobs but I somehow felt I was not his cup of tea, with my short pins and unremarkable face. I always seemed to be the odd-girl-out in long lines of sixties beauties, with bum-length blonde hair, endless legs and matching berets and dresses of fluffy angora.

Anyway, I rang James from Worthing, told him I was back from Killarney (where he'd never encouraged me to go!) and hoped he would go to work for me.

Meanwhile County Hall came through with a couple of supply jobs to take me through October.

I went back to London and to celebrate the coming injection to my finances, I bought a huge jumper, red-and-beige kind of check. Not angora but definitely fluffy!

One of the teaching jobs was very brief, thank God. Two days in a Battersea nursery class where the two to three year olds were only marginally more scared of me than I of them. I had absolutely no idea how to handle twenty toddlers, no clue as to what a limited attention span little ones have. I'd exhausted my entire repertoire of inspiration after fifteen minutes.

'Where's the other lady?' they queried hopelessly.

Thanks to the good graces of the infant helper who came in at dinner-time and took pity on me, I muddled through. Somehow. It was with huge relief that I trundled out for a week at a Hackney secondary modern school. My first lesson was forty-six fifteen-year-old girls for a double lesson of country dancing. Now, as you know from Killarney, I've always hated dancing and in particular country dancing. So it seemed did my little charges.

'We don' wanna do farking country dancing.'

'That's for cants.'

'I ain' farkin moving.'

I soon decided compromise was the better part of discipline, especially as they were mostly bigger than me, and I suggested that as I was far from expert in the country-dancing field, we should do 'Drama' with a capital 'D'.

I divided them into groups of six and gave them each a kind of loose situation, heavily based on TV programmes of the day. Together we cobbled six playlets in lesson one and acted and voted on them in lesson two. The girls were wonderful! Loud, but wonderful.

Murder and sex featured heavily on the agenda even in the *Coronation Street* prototype. As the stories unfolded I looked at these people I was supposed to be teaching. I was completely ignorant of real life. I was educated but I was innocent. In a curious way, chatting to these girls, several of whom I later learned were already 'on the game', I felt more of a virgin than I had before going to Ireland.

I enjoyed my time at Hackney, teaching everything from PE to physics. I was only ever one step ahead of the pupils and usually relied heavily on a bright child in subjects of which I was totally ignorant. I'd inherited a natural authority from the family I suppose, all teachers, so discipline was never a problem. But the kids loved to wind me up.

To guard against waste in the school, toilet paper was handed out by the teacher on request, a humiliating and embarrassing arrangement for both parties. One day a particular boy seemed to be making more than the usual trips to the bog and I suspected he was in and out for a quick fag. After about the fifth request I said to him, exasperated: 'What on earth are you doing in there?'

He flung his hand across his chest and arranged his spiky face into an expression more of sorrow than anger, and murmured: 'Oh, miss, 'ow can you ask?'

The class nearly wet themselves. What could I do?

Hammersmith 1952–3

I hated this new school at first. They treat you like a baby, the big girls, and some of them try to intimidate you, especially the Lower Fourth. That's one year above me. They run very hard and close past you on the stairs and sometimes they giggle behind you and you don't know why. Some of them smell of hotpot too – under the arms.

Anyway – it's not too bad now – getting better. I've forced myself to stop being shy, because it doesn't get you anywhere.

I did it during a history lesson on the paleolithic age. Miss Pond was teaching us cuneiform writing and I suddenly decided not to be shy. I'm not quite sure why it happened then. It may have been because history makes you feel very small and whatever you do is very tiny and not important so you might as well do something, because nobody will notice anyway. And being unshy is better than being shy.

Things are better now too because I've got a really good friend, Jenny. She's very tall and blonde and she's a very good dancer and had been in real shows as a babe. Her mother and father are lovely and I sometimes stay with them in Peckham. It's very peaceful there, only the three of them. And Jenny has a very beautiful bedroom, pink and lace. And in the corner is her vanity case that she keeps her ballet things in. I would love a vanity case.

Things are better too because I wrote a really good poem.

I gave it to Mother Morris who teaches us English, and is our form teacher, and she said she wanted Mrs Talbot to look at it for the school magazine.

Funnily enough I met Mrs Talbot on the train then. I go on the Circle Line from Victoria, and she got on at Earls Court. I was a bit embarrassed because she sat next to me and started talking about the poem, and said it had a touch of genius. She'd read my flood poem too, but didn't like it as much.

'Say it for me now. The "Unknown Warrior" one.'
Oh God.
'OK.' I coughed a bit. 'To An Unknown Warrior':

> *He lies at last the brave one,*
> *Who fought until the end,*
> *Till sweat and blood did pour forth*
> *From wounds that would not mend.*
>
> *He lies, not in a coffin dark*
> *And sweet with fading flowers.*
> *But on the grey wide battlefield*
> *Still wet with morning showers.*
>
> *No mourner weeps about his death*
> *No flowers grow o'er his head.*
> *But peace has come to him at last*
> *Now that his blood is shed.*
>
> *So God the good, who made all things*
> *Grow grasses straight and tall.*
> *And meadow flowers about his head*
> *To make a funeral pall.*

'Brilliant,' said Mrs Talbot, and closed her eyes. I couldn't think of anything else to say, and I didn't know whether to move or not, so I just took out my maths book and started to read it.

It wasn't until November that I noticed I hadn't had a period for a couple of months.

In fact it was Tony who first commented that my breasts looked a bit different, fuller, with more marked blue veins. We'd been lying on my bed in a companionable heap watching the November afternoon change imperceptibly into evening over the park.

Since leaving Ireland our relationship had inevitably become less intense. We were no longer joined at the hip twenty-four hours a day. Our friends and interests were quite different and although we each tried to bring the other into our London lives, it didn't seem to happen. Curiously now we had the freedom to spend the whole night together – no landladies, no creaking boards – we very rarely did.

Occasionally Tony might stay over till Sunday, which was a kind of hiatus period in the weekly round of hopes raised and dashed on the work front.

Marie and I really loved it when people stayed. We did the full bit. Old-fashioned Sunday dinner – meat and three veg – and lit a proper fire.

I suppose it was playing house really, putting whoever the current boyfriend was in the domestic picture and seeing how he looked. I'm sure we would both have denied it, Marie and I, but there must have been in us then, that subconscious female thing that surfaces in the twenties – not 'Where am I going?' but 'With whom? Who will reflect those most secret hopes and opinions? Who won't laugh at them?'

At that time, I was only just beginning to consider that I didn't necessarily need a man's approval to accomplish something.

Tony was always funny and warm and joined in with a good heart; but there was in him an ephemeral quality that would not take kindly to ritual and sameness. He was the South Wind, invigorating, disturbing – moving on, not to be contained.

I felt in him a desire to distance himself from me and I think I wanted it too, but was afraid there was nothing to replace it. He was always very straight, didn't conceal or manipulate, simply spoke his thoughts and looked for my reaction.

We decided to make a gentle separation, still going to the odd film or having a meal together. But to remove the obligation of regularity from our relationship. Also Tony was feeling physically run down and had started consulting a homeopath, fairly avant-garde twenty-eight years ago.

I think the pace of Killarney had taken more out of us than we thought, and we both needed recharging time.

Lying on the bed that evening, I looked at the blue veins with a new eye. I must have noticed them before but thought that was part of the new mature me, without my virginity. It had never entered my head that I could get pregnant; nor Tony's for that matter. We must have been real innocents, idiots maybe. After he left that evening I paced up and down the flat, looking in various mirrors for a new perspective. Was I fatter? Did I crave anything? Weren't you supposed to have irrational desire for strange combinations of food? One of Gabe's friends had an insatiable appetite for chutney sandwiches. And I remember Mama saying she always became addicted to ginger biscuits, when she was expecting all of us. I had none of these. Maybe it was just the upheaval, physical and emotional, of a first lover. It was, after all, a major turning point in my life; the decision to 'give' myself to someone, a mixture of heady delight and deep-seated guilt. I had, after all, broken the rules I promised to keep. 'Thou shalt not commit adultery.' I'd convinced myself that the cessation of my menstrual flow was nothing more than a psychosomatic block, when Marie came in and I told her my worries.

Marie, who'd never had a regular cycle in her life, reassured me. It was probably all due to the travel and the changes that had taken place in my life. She suggested I went to the doctor to put my mind at rest, and he'd give me something to restore the rhythm. I didn't want to go to our local GP who'd known me since childhood. God knows why now. Dear Dr Golomb, he certainly wouldn't have gone rushing into the streets shouting, 'This girl is not a virgin.'

It's funny when you break your own set of rules, how obsessed you become with the idea that everybody is absolutely fascinated by this. I remember, in the shops, scrutinizing George Hall the greengrocer, and thinking, Is he different towards me? Can he tell?

'And three pounds of sprouts please, George.'

'Right, anything else? Got some nice oranges.'

No jokes. He knows. He disapproves.

Marie remembered the name of an Egyptian doctor in Chelsea, who she'd been to when she first came to England. I looked up the number and made an appointment for the next day, said I was from the north, a student, gave my own name as a temporary patient; this in the days before computerized patient lists.

The next day around four o'clock, I caught the 137 over the river, and went to the surgery off the King's Road. It was a gloomy evening and the waiting-room, though clean, had dim lighting and a generally disenchanted air. I registered with the receptionist as a temporary patient and filled in the card 'Paula Collings', giving an address in Lincoln that I vaguely remembered from someone at college. This was the first of the lies.

Doctor Benoub was a paternal looking man with an unsmiling face. He took notes about dates and enquired whether I had a sexual partner and what form of contraception I used.

'None,' I said.

'The young man?'

'Nothing.'

'Isn't he a responsible young man? Are you not responsible people?'

I didn't know how to reply.

110

'I didn't think it would happen. We didn't think.'
Feeble. Hopeless.

He gave me an internal. Simple words. Not then. I'd never had one. Lying rigid on the couch without my knickers or my dignity, while he fiddled about, not unkindly, making little noises to himself.

When he finished, he sat me down and wrote a prescription.

'Six pills – two a day for three days. If you're pregnant they won't affect you, and won't harm the baby. If you're not, your period should start within a week. Meanwhile leave a sample of urine in the bathroom on your way out. Come and see me next week.'

The longest week of my life.

After a couple of days I felt familiar burning twinges in the pit of my stomach. Hallelujah, I knew that feeling. Twelve hours' burn, then the curse. Blessed curse. I felt really cheered. Everything felt normal now. I was pale, drained, backachy, and full of hope. Marie and I went out for a curry in Chelsea and walked back over the bridge. It was a beautiful night, quite cold and starry. We leaned over the side for a while, watching the lights of Albert Bridge down the river, dancing in the night water.

You can't do that any more now. Sometimes I feel absolutely desolate that the London night no longer belongs to us, that you can't take a night walk without inviting at best the attentions of a kerb crawler or even the police. At worst something much more terrifying and final.

The week trundled by, the nagging pains came and went and on Wednesday I went back to Dr Benoub.

I sat in front of him while he looked through his notes.

'Yes. Any period?'

'No. Not yet.'

'Yes.' He looked up and stared straight at me, not unkindly. 'Well, your pregnancy test is positive.'

'Oh.' Nothing to say. What could I say?

'I think you should discuss this with your young man and then come back when you've decided where you want to have the baby.'

I stood up and thanked him, shaking his hand as if he'd just turned me down for a job, and walked through the waiting ones and home on the 137.

Marie was in when I got back, getting ready for a party we'd been invited to. It promised to be a really good one, given by some old mates from college, Roger, Pete and Les. Uncomplicated company and great party givers.

I told Marie the news. She was as shocked as I. It was unimaginable. We sat drinking tea while Marie lit the fire to warm our spirits. I didn't in the least feel like partygoing. I felt nine foot wide with 'fallen woman' tattooed across my forehead.

Because they were such good guys, we both felt bad about letting them down, not turning up to the party. We decided to go. It was an alternative to sitting in the flat, wondering what on earth to do.

I made a sandwich for the two of us. You never knew if there'd be anything to eat. Gabe wasn't in till later and we listened to the radio while we put our make-up on, tucked up by the fire. I looked awful. Puffy. Plain. Hopeless. More mascara.

'. . . is a newsflash.'

I went over my lips again, more pale pink. More ghostlike.

'News is coming through of a shooting.'

Spit into the Max Factor block. Pull up those eyelashes.

'News is coming through of a shooting in Dallas, Texas.'

Maybe a bit more backcombing – up with the waterfall of hair, backcomb the top knot.

'We are receiving unconfirmed reports that John Kennedy has been shot.'

Marie, arrested in the middle of drawing an eyeline. My hands fixed above my head.

'Reports are coming through that the President of the United States, John Kennedy, has been shot in Dallas, Texas.'

I looked at Marie. She turned up the radio. I switched on the television.

'President John Kennedy has been shot in Dallas, Texas, along with Governor Connally, as their motorcade passed through the town. We do not yet know the extent of their injuries.'

Throughout the night we sat round the television, joined by Gabe, when she came home, as the gravity of the situation emerged. History has tried to reveal Kennedy to us as fallible, womanizing, an adulterer of questionable papish stock.

But then he was golden. In that time, for that time, he was a president of unique energy, of charisma. We were devastated.

As the truth became known, Catholics all round the world wanted to unite in some way. Around 2 a.m. we rang Westminster Cathedral to ask what services were being held in his memory. We had a very curious and cold response. I don't know whether it was a priest or a layman. Maybe we were the nine hundredth phone call he'd received, but he replied: 'The next round of applause will be at 10 a.m. tomorrow morning.'

I rang Mama to say good night and wasn't it terrible? They were all still awake in Worthing, watching the awful pictures over and over again.

'We didn't eat tonight. No one felt like eating,' said Mama.

'No, we didn't. Half a sandwich.'

'I think I'd spoiled my appetite anyway,' Mama said. 'I've been eating ginger biscuits all day. I've got a craving for ginger biscuits.'

* * *

Well here's a surprise. Mama's had a baby. We've got a baby sister. She was so huge we all thought she was a boy. But no. Another girl. Claire, eleven years younger than Gabe. She's a Coronation baby. The Queen was crowned and everybody watched the Coronation on television.

Dada gave in and bought one. Yippee! And Mama gave in and bought what she said she never would – red, white and blue decorations – and we did up the balcony till it looked like a battleship. Red, white and blue bunting, streamers, flags, balloons. Everywhere.

Then for the holidays Gabe and I went to St Margaret's Bay with Maurice and Auntie and Mama and Dada joined us when Claire was two weeks old. It was a bit squashed in the chalet, only two bedrooms, but it's a beautiful place. I loved waking up very early and climbing out of the window while everyone's still asleep and lying in the long grass, watching the sun come up.

Maurice and Auntie are moving to a furnished flat after the summer, till one comes up along the drive. It's a bit too crowded for us all now, with the new baby in our place.

Summer 1954

Dada's very fed up. I went from second to fourteenth in class this year. Dada says it's because of the television. I told him the work's much harder but I think he may be right. We're going to be limited from now on. Bugger it.

We had a good summer though. We rented a house in Cliftonville which is only about ten minutes from Margate and Dreamland. I absolutely love Dreamland. It's a huge fair a hundred times bigger than New Brighton, and there's loads of different rides and machines.

Little Phil came down for a couple of weeks so it was like old times the three of us on the shore and at the fairground.

We're not allowed to stay out at night though. We have to be back by eight. Damnation. That's when it gets going. Mama says maybe next year. I want to stay out now.

Jenny left school this year. She's going to Pitman's. I'll really, really miss her. I don't think she wants to be a secretary. I think she'll probably be a professional dancer in the end.

No best friend in September though. Horrible feeling.

December 1954

I love winter. I can hide out in my room, read for hours into the still watches of the night. I'm in the little room near the front door, that used to be the playroom. Mama says it'll be good for study to be on my own, now I'm at the Grammar School. She lights a fire in there and I settle down to work after my tea.

After they're all asleep though I keep the fire going and listen to the wireless. I've got my own crystal set now. I love listening to Radio Luxembourg or Hilversum because they've got lots of American music. There's a song I love that's on all the time now. 'On the Waterfront'. It's from a film by Elia Kazan. That's the man who did A Tree Grows in Brooklyn. *Best film ever. The music's very sad and it goes with the book I'm reading,* The Story of Mrs Murphy. *It's about a man who's a drunk but his wife really loves him, and he keeps promising to be good and then isn't. At the beginning of the book it's got a quotation:*

> *Booze is your wife*
> *Booze, that's who you're married to.*

I'm not sure if it's suitable for me so I read it under the covers by torch. It's all about New York. I love the sadness of it.

We're allowed to read quite a lot. One funny thing. Dada wouldn't let us read Enid Blyton. Said it'd make our brains go soft. I used to love The Magic Faraway Tree *though. Read it on the quiet!*

When I told Tony the news that I really was pregnant, he was terrific. He said more or less straightaway that one solution was that we could get married. I know he meant it although it must have been the last thing in the world he really wanted to do. As for me, I said, 'Thank you but no, thank you.' I don't really know why I continued to see Tony, because from that moment I started to shut him out of any future plans I may have had. In my arrogance I told him that this pregnancy was my problem, my concern, and mine alone. I suppose we continued to see each other because I needed to talk to someone and he and Marie were the only people who knew.

In my singleminded self-sufficiency I never considered that he, as a man, might have real feelings about being a father. I suppose I had a horror of him being tied to me by a sense of duty and rather than let that even raise its head, I rejected him first.

Somewhere, too, there was a wild hope that it might all be a mistake and that next week everything would be back to normal, and I'd be young again and with this ostrich-like attitude I continued my life trying to disregard the heavy burden on my soul and in my stomach.

I took increasing amounts of supply work as a teacher in a variety of schools. During a two-week spell at a very poor junior school, I found myself in the headmaster's study for a bit of advice. One of my ten year olds had walked out of the building after I told him off. The head, who was an extremely gentle and compassionate man, told me that I had to be extra careful in handling some of the children because they had such rough lives at home.

'A lot of them have never known their fathers. Jacky, who ran out of school, has a different man in the house

116

every few months, trying to tell him what to do. So you have to be a bit understanding when you're disciplining him.'

I felt ashamed and terrible for more reasons than he knew.

The first time I went down to Worthing after I knew I was expecting you, I wore a skinny sweater and a tight skirt half-hoping maybe that someone would look and say, 'Are you having a baby?' and I would say 'yes' and the problem would be thrown into the family pot.

We've all always been intensely loyal to each other, our family. Much given to inter-relative scraps and shouts but instantly able to close ranks if an outsider wrongs any of us.

Everyone was there that weekend. Frank was home from America, doing business in Europe for a month. Gabe followed me down late on Friday night after work. Although we were living together, I hadn't shared my secret with Gabe. We led very different lives, had different kinds of friends and I was afraid that she would be horrified by my promiscuity.

Maurice met me at the station as he so often did for so many people throughout the years. Always the willing chauffeur at the drop of a hat.

The wonderful thing about going to Worthing was that everyone was always so pleased to see us, so welcoming. Although that house had never really been my home, all the components of home were there. Mama, Dada, Auntie, Maurice, Frank and Claire – all the constants of my childhood still together. It was still a wonderful place to go and abdicate responsibility, to become a child again.

I remember that weekend as being particularly lovely. We all bundled into the kitchen while Mama cooked, Frank making little drinks to keep the cook going, someone peeling the veg, someone making big fat cheese-and-onion sandwiches. Late at night lots of music and talking, word games. Nobody went to bed much before dawn.

There was a lot of news for Frank to catch up on. Both Auntie and Maurice had given up the idea of working locally and now commuted to London with Dada; Maurice had nearly been made Head of Science, Mama in her Goring school was now Mistress in Charge of Religion and Moral Discipline. Everything was rosy.

In the midst of this Claire, then ten, ploughed her own furrow, mad about horses, spending every spare moment mucking out at the stables, escaping the disciplinarians no doubt.

Everyone said how good I looked that weekend, a bit thinner after the summer in Ireland, but good. I wanted to leap up in the small hours of Sunday morning and shout, 'I'm not thin. I'm pregnant. I'm going to have a baby.' But I couldn't. I was always the good child, the good girl. I was no trouble. I made tea; vacated my bed for visiting sailors; worked hard, passed my exams; did funny voices, made them laugh. Started a career, made them proud.

Here they were after a lifetime of cheerful struggle, settled and peaceful and secure. How could I drop that bombshell on that contented hearth? I couldn't do it.

Back in London on Monday there was an unexpected flurry of activity on the phone. For most aspirant actors Monday is yet another stretch of silence, after the lull of the weekend, but there was always the outside chance of a surprise. This was just such a day. James rang from the agency with not one but two interviews for me, both that week.

The first, on Wednesday, was for a commercial for Topic, the chocolate bar. I went to the ad agency wearing a bright red A-line dress, woollen with no sleeves. I looked OK. I'd never been for a commercial and was flabbergasted by the number of people who were there to look me over. About twelve people were seated on one side of a conference table while I sat in solitary unease on the other. There were two 'talkers' who asked me what I'd done and if I liked Topic. Like it. I adore it. Then, while I said 'Mmmm Topic' in several different ways, the watchers leaned back in their chairs and surveyed my indifferent legs and my A-cup bust.

After several pieces of direction from the talkers, I suddenly came up with a rather suggestive reading of 'Mmmm Topic'. They all fell about laughing and buzzing and I felt quite cheered. Then they said goodbye and we'll let you know.

The next day James rang to say they had narrowed the choice to two girls and would test us both next week and, glory of glories, I would be paid for the test! Later the same day a nice wardrobe mistress arranged to go shopping for a dress.

I was a bit worried when I met her that she'd notice my lump but I kept my slip on and all she said was I was 'deceptive' and settled for a rather dreary number in an unremarkable shade of red.

On Friday I went for the second interview. James had managed to get me seen for a documentary film for the Spastics Association, starring John Hurt, an actor I've always loved. There were two small parts for girls in a club scene and I saw the director and read well. He wouldn't make a decision till next week.

On Tuesday morning, very early, I took a train to Beaconsfield Studios for my Topic test. My call was for 7.30 a.m. so I was up at sparrows' fart, doing my hair, now shorter in the kind of 'Cleopatra' shape of the day, straight fringed and with two long points moving up towards the cheekbones. It had all disintegrated a bit by the time I arrived at the studio and my face felt fat and splobby.

I was taken into make-up and met my rival, Joy, a really pretty girl with short black hair in a soft, natural, urchin cut. She was very friendly, a model, who'd made several commercials.

We were taken on to the set and shown the script. A bit more than 'Mmmm Topic' it turned out, sitting on a high stool: 'I've got a secret, I want to tell you about. It's' – unwrapping bar – 'chocolatey and hazelnutty and' – bite – 'mmm Topic.'

Joy did her run through first, a rather flat delivery, but prettily, and unwrapped her bar with consummate ease and long manicured fingernails culminating in a delicate bite of chocolate.

I thought I might improve on interpretation, but was a non-starter in the fingernails stakes. I delivered my line quite winningly I thought, and scruffled out my Topic bar before putting it slowly to my lips and murmuring 'Mmmm – Topic' as sexily as I had in the interview.

'No, darling, that's much too much, over the top. Make it more surprised and delighted.'

Ah well.

We each did another run through and then the director decided to go for a take, first Joy, then me.

Joy did three immaculate takes in fifteen minutes, looking quite lovely in her cream knitted dress, and everyone seemed well pleased.

It was quite hot in the set by now and the make-up girl came to press even more powder on my caked face and lacquered my hair into place against my cheeks.

Joy was a tough act to follow so I decided to go for bright and cheeky (although I felt far from either), sensing that cool and sexy was not my forte.

On the first take I thought I was pretty OK, a bit stiff-faced from fear, but lively in delivery and more or less smooth in deliverance.

'Good. Another one for luck. Try to make the sliding out of the bar and up to the mouth more of a continous movement.'

Take Two was OK, smooth movement. A bit too

suggestive again on 'Mmm Topic'. Take Three was pretty good but a bit lacking in pleasure on biting the bar. Take Four, a bit too much pleasure on biting the bar. On Take Five my hand stuck as I pulled out the bar, my hands were getting a bit hot by now. Take Six, my hand slipped again. The prop man came in and powdered my hand. Take Seven, no good, the powder came off on the bar. Take Eight, my hand stuck again. Take Nine, the bar slipped out and on to the floor. Take Ten I want to die. Take Eleven, an electrician walks by, talking to his mate.

'Well, I know which one I'd have. No contest.'

Take Twelve, boom shadow. Take Thirteen, I did it. I am no longer bright, far from cheeky and not in the least suggestive. I am rigid with anxiety, sweating, fat-stomached, stilted and joyless but I got the bar out of the wrapper and into my mouth in one smooth movement.

'OK, studio, that's a wrap. Thank you very much.'

Needless to say, I never heard another word. Joy was the Topic Girl for at least a year. Good luck to her.

I began to think that week that I was temperamentally unsuited to the fickle world of showbiz. Killarney had lulled me into a false sense of security with its supportive atmosphere. Just when I had learned the joy of the profession, just when I felt I really could be an actor, make it my way of life, here I was, back in London, the real hub of the profession, a complete failure. I'd been fooling myself. It was all very well playing nightly to packed houses in Ireland but in the real world where competition was hot and the stakes were high, I was a no hoper. I couldn't follow through in a 'big' job like the Topic campaign.

I was feeling really low by Sunday, when suddenly Tony rang up inviting me to a special night out on Monday. We were going to a club called the Blue Angel where a brilliant new American comedian had a two-week engagement.

On Monday night I poured myself into the red audition dress, high, high heels and shiny ear-rings. I squirted myself liberally with L'Emeraude, wrapped myself in my winter coat, a mottled grey-and-black affair with a huge pouter pigeon collar made of fluffy fur from some unidentified animal. It was meant to be tightly belted but I thought this might betray my thickening waist so I kind of clutched it to me. I looked like a struggling hooker but I felt great as I click-clacked up the steps of the Piccadilly tube to meet Tony.

We got to the club early to get a good seat in a rosy little alcove, and I took out a packet of coloured Sobrani cocktail cigarettes to make me feel chic and sophisticated. We drank pretty drinks in pretty colours and nibbled cocktail savouries while a good jazz trio played cool stuff. The place was not full. There were quite a few empty tables and those that were occupied were heavily monopolized by pissed Debs' Delights, and a few Middle Easterners with pretty blonde girls. A few of us danced a bit on the tiny floor. Then around ten-thirty the band did a kind of 'hurry hurry' theme to introduce the comedian: 'Ladies and gentlemen, please welcome' – cymbals, drum roll – 'Woody – Allen!'

And we all cheered.

On came this little guy, melancholic, weedy, scarcely older than us, and introduced us first hand to a kind of deprecating, self-flagellating, introverted humour that was completely new to us. It took Tony and me two minutes to tune in to his style and then we loved him but I think that night we were in a minority. There can be nothing worse than playing to an audience of piss-artists who are leagues away from your culture, for whom the live performer is nothing more than an intrusion on the serious business of drinking and pulling the birds. God knows, he gave them everything. I remember him at one point walking on the empty tables to better reach his audience. I wanted to shout: Come over here. Play to this little pink alcove. Don't waste your energy on drunks.

I wonder if he remembers that night. As well as introducing me to his talent, it also did something else for me. I thought if someone that good can have a rough experience, maybe failure to deliver the goods in a Topic ad is not exactly the end of the world. Here's lookin' at you, Mr A.

Summer 1955

Well, I did get another best friend, Janet Walker, who is the quietest and wittiest person in the world. The wonderful thing about her is we like exactly the same things. We love English and music and hate science and sport. On hockey days we try to have bad ankles or bronchitis or anything to preserve us from all that running up and down and cracking each other on the legs. I bandaged my leg three weeks running but I didn't think I dare push my luck again.

It's not so bad now in the summer, whacking the tennis ball over the net. At least we get our arms and legs brown.

Something else, we've got boyfriends. We met them at the Junior Drama League when we did a course there.

We've been to the pictures with them and on days out to Syon Park, and once to the country. That was a marvellous day.

It was a very old-fashioned kind of day. Janet and I made the picnic and they brought the drinks and we all went on the train together.

Everything smelled very warm and drowsy, lots of bees humming around. We held hands quite a lot and Janet's boy, Andrew, put his hand inside her blouse. I wish James had but he was a bit shy and started whistling and picking flowers. He was like that before too. Once when he kissed me after the pictures, he put his tongue in my mouth, quite far; it felt funny at first but I quite liked it. Then he went very red

*and said good night quickly, and marched off with his hands
in his pockets.*

*We have good times, though, Janet and I, and we each
know what the other's thinking. Sometimes when a teacher
does something that makes us laugh, we only have to move
say a pencil a quarter of an inch to the right and each of us
knows what the other one's saying: 'See that – hysterical.'*

That's a best friend.

Towards the end of that week I had a call from James. I'd
got the documentary with John Hurt! It was only two
days but it was quite a nice little scene, to be shot in a
West End club in two weeks' time. A film! I had only
worked on video. Shooting 'a film' seemed wonderful
and glamorous. James said the production company
would be in touch with me about a medical next week. A
medical? I didn't know what he was talking about.

'You have to have a medical for the insurance.'

I died a small death. I would be discovered, found out,
rumbled. I saw the £12 fee disappearing before my eyes.
Wealth beyond the dreams of avarice.

'OK. Fine. Bye, James.'

I put the phone down and sat in a heap till Marie came
in.

'What can I do?' Hopeless and helpless.

Marie dragged me back from the Slough of Despond.

'You don't look at all pregnant. Not even stripped
down.'

We looked at me in bra and pants from every angle. I
felt huge but actually I didn't look fat at all.

'It's probably such a brief medical,' said Marie.
'Heart, blood pressure, lungs, urine test.'

'Urine test. That's it. I can't do it. He'll know.'

Despair sat amongst us once again, then Gabe came in
and the subject had to be dropped.

I often thought later what a burden I placed on Marie
during that period of my life. There she was, my great

friend, almost a member of my family, constantly mixing with them but weighed down by my secret. Concealing on my behalf, lying on my behalf; not fair on her. I can never thank her enough for her unquestioning support.

As we lay awake that night in the bedroom we shared, she had a brilliant, daring and hysterically funny idea.

'Why don't you take some of my pee?'

'What?'

'Why don't you take a specimen of my pee? Tell the doctor you thought you had to bring one.'

It was a wonderful idea. I might just get away with it.

The following Wednesday I set off to the insurance doctor with a thumping heart, and a Gordon's gin bottle that Marie had obligingly filled to the brim.

'Marie, what can I say?'

In his consulting rooms, I stripped to my pants and held my breath while he listened to my heart and lungs, took my blood pressure and looked at my eyes and ears. Nearly finished. Then, 'Could you just lie down on the couch a moment?'

I did.

He then felt my breasts and passed a practised hand over my lower abdomen.

'A little swollen here. Full bladder?'

Faintly 'Yes. No – I'm about to have my period.'

'Aah, yes.'

Does he believe me?

'Now if you'd like to get dressed, then pop into the cloakroom and do a urine specimen for me.'

Deep breath.

'OK,' I said brightly. 'But I do sometimes have a bit of a problem with that. I get nervous and sort of seize up. I'll go and try but I did bring a sample I did at home.'

I offered the brimming gin bottle. Here's one I prepared earlier. Oh God.

'Oh, that's fine. That'll do fine. Just leave it with me.'

I can go. I can't believe it. Have I got away with it? I

dressed and fled out of the smart building on to the 137 home to wait for the bombshell to drop.

But none did. The next thing I got was a script, a call time and instructions to wear a casual disco outfit for the two days' shooting.

A week later I found myself meeting the girl playing my mate and finding that she was funny, easy to know and a smashing actress. She was tall and blonde. I was short and dark. Mutt and Jeff we were. Her name was Wendy Richard.

I really enjoyed those two days. We didn't have a great deal to do, dance a bit, laugh a bit and then a little scene in which we are first embarrassed, and then supportive when confronted by a spastic boy who wants to join the club. Simplistic stuff but well intentioned. John Hurt, already well established as an actor, and playing the 'star' role of the young man with cerebral palsy, was really kind and good to us small-part players.

I never saw the film but I felt truthful in it, and more important for my shattered psyche, I felt 'valued', a useful member of the company. Fuck Topic. This was the real stuff.

Summer 1955/II

This has been the most fantastic summer. It started really unpromising. We're very short of dough because Mama's only part-time now. Stan Boniface minds Claire in the mornings while Mama teaches. He's a postman on nights and Mama teaches his daughter.

Anyway Dad said we can't afford to rent a house at the seaside so we'd have days out. I was really disappointed but I knew it couldn't be helped.

It's funny being in London in the summer. The swings smell even dirtier than usual. Not that I go on them any more but we take Claire. She loved the 'swingers'.

I got a season ticket to the Sculpture Exhibition in the far end of the Park. I like the statues, especially the little bronze girl, but I also like the peace. I take a picnic and a book, and stretch out by the laurel bush in a little corner.

Suddenly, in the beginning of the holidays, someone asked Mama if she could take some French students for a couple of weeks. They weren't happy in their digs.

'It's a very nice quiet girl of thirteen and her little brother.' Not quite true!

Well! It was a nice quiet girl, Anne-Marie le Douarin, who became my real friend but also huge Loïc, not her brother, living with us officially and Alain and Hervé, spending most of their time with us unofficially. We had a wonderful time, Dada was in his element, with all those people he could coach in English and I loved speaking French with them.

We went all round London – all the visitor things and I roped in Jenny. The boys adored her. She looks so good now, beautiful, full dresses with halter necks. I've got one too, but it doesn't look quite the same. Anne-Marie just wore a T-shirt and skirt but she looks incredibly chic. Maybe I'll try that casual look. I don't think I've got style though. We went swimming a lot too, and it's funny how you enjoy your own town much more when you see it with a stranger.

Next year I'm going to France to stay with Anne-Marie, I can hardly wait. I wished it could be now. Hey ho.

After the French had gone home, Dada said we'd have a day out at Cliftonville because we know it. So we made food and drinks and packed the car the night before with towels and rugs and deckchairs, and set off very early in the morning. We five, and Auntie.

We arrived on the beach really early and bagged a good spot while Dada unloaded in the car park. Then we got a couple more deckchairs from the man and set up our patch. Mama made a bit of a tent for Claire with towels across the deckchairs, in case she wanted a sleep, and then we all changed into our costumes in the Ladies.

We were starving by then so Dada got a tray of tea from the beach café, and the man remembered us from last year.

It was an absolutely glorious day. The sun shone and shone. We swam and played with Claire and had a game of cricket with the family next to us.

About seven, Mama said we'd have to think of moving soon. It was still really hot and we didn't want to go. Just then Dada came back from the car park. He'd been talking to a family who had a tent in the back of their van. They were staying the night, sleeping in the car park.

Dada looked at Mama and Auntie.

'Shall we stay? Shall we stay the night?'

At first the ladies weren't sure, they had no toothbrushes, no knickers. Where would we sleep?

'Please, Mum, let's stay.' Gabe and I begged and nagged.

In the end they said yes. Madness but yes. Dada went off and got toothbrushes and soap and a few bits to eat, while we tried to sort out how to sleep. In the end we flattened out all the seats in the car to make a big bed for Auntie and Mama and Claire. Dada would sleep in a deckchair and Gabe and I on a pile of towels with a rug.

About eight, Dada went for fish and chips and got the café to fill up our thermoses and the other family had got a fire going so we all sat round together and chatted and sang songs, till we went to sleep.

The next morning we were a bit stiff when we woke up but it was another wonderful day.

We washed in the sea, and cleaned our teeth when the toilets opened at eight o'clock. We had fruit and tea and bread and butter for breakfast.

And later on in the morning we got bacon sandwiches from the beach café.

By lunch-time everyone decided we should stay in the car park for another couple of days or as long as we could.

Mama phoned Maurice with lengthy instructions about bedding and nighties and knickers and poor Mau obligingly agreed to bring everything down.

He arrived in the late afternoon with a mountain of stuff including sleeping-bags borrowed from Mrs Iv. and a camping stove, with a bag of easy-cook food: bacon, sausages, bread and fruit.

That night two more families had joined us, one of them a big gang from Bermondsey who had a portable radio. So not only did we have a huge fire but also music to dance to. It was very friendly – all of us chatting and helping each other out with the odd bit of milk or bread. The father of the Bermondsey family was an old hand at car-park camping, and with great savvy had a whip-round for the toilet attendant to leave the doors unlocked so we could wash properly and use the lavs at night.

It was a wonderful five days. Funny isn't it how something unexpected can turn out to be one of your best holidays? I loved waking in the open air and falling asleep with starshine on my head.

More families joined us as the week went on. Then Big Brother stepped in and spoiled it all. First notices went up in the toilets: NO WASHING OF CLOTHES.

Then a big notice went up on the car park: NO OVERNIGHT CAMPING.

So we all said bugger it and goodbye and maybe next year.

So back to London. School soon. But next year for me, France! I can hardly wait.

Christmas was nearly upon us, and I would spend it, of course, with the family. I had no work, neither acting nor teaching. Most schools were about to break up, and I could have gone down to Worthing at any time, but I decided to minimize my time there, and therefore the risk of my being discovered. We'd never been a very private family. Bathrooms were always places for multiple occupation and gossip, and I'd almost certainly be in Auntie's double bed to sleep, so the fewer nights I spent there the better. I was sad about that.

I've always absolutely loved Christmas for every aspect

of the feast. I love the choosing of presents, the shopping for food, the preparations, decorating the house. I love the carols on the radio, on the doorstep, the inevitable tacky Christmas pop song. I love Midnight Mass with its heady aroma of incense and faint whiffs of alcohol. I love the endless nights when we are no longer chained to time and timetable, the utterly silent street on Christmas morning.

As a large, mostly adult, family, we periodically tried to put a moratorium on presents for everyone from everyone but it never really worked. For one thing it was no fun for Claire to be the sole recipient of everyone's bounty and for another we all missed the giving of something, however small.

I had a great idea that year for Claire. Instead of one good present, I decided to buy a waste-paper bin and fill it with jolly junky bits. Mama was always saying that half of what children received at Christmas was unwrapped and broken or forgotten within a few days. Christmas rubbish she called it. So I decided to aim really low, cut out the middleman, and give her a binful of Christmas rubbish! I kept my eyes open for really silly cheap toys and notions that would be fun to unwrap and play with for a while and then be thrown away or forgotten.

I had a great time trekking round Clapham Junction and the Latchmere filling my bin with trash. A mouth-organ, jars of beads, a plastic snowstorm, little books, dolls, china horse and foal (made in Hong Kong), a pink plastic handbag.

I wrapped everything individually in different packages from a mixed pack of Christmas paper. By the time I'd finished there must have been about fifty little presents, in an inviting jumble in the bin.

For the men I chose good books, for the ladies soap and talc, boring and predictable but I'd exhausted my inspiration on Claire.

Maurice, kind heart that he was, drove up the day

before Christmas Eve to give Gabe and me a lift down. It was wonderful not to have to battle our way on the train. Just stuff all our bits in the boot and enjoy the ride.

Arriving in the clear cold of early evening, the house shone a welcome from every window. I could see the Christmas tree in the window of the living-room, glowing with fairy lights and decorated with enthusiastic overkill by Claire. I've always admired really tasteful trees with white pin lights and just the right amount of subdued Victorian tree ornaments in gentle colours and soft gold. We never quite managed to achieve that! Lights too round the door. I could see Auntie in the far end of the dining-room, going through sheet music by the piano. We knocked on the window and rang the bell. Dada answered and we piled into the kitchen, dumping bags in the hall.

Every year some drink or other became a family favourite for the duration of the festivities. That year it was Warninck's Advocaat and lemonade, pretty harmless stuff. I couldn't help thinking it was quite good for a baby, all that egg and cream.

Christmas Eve the next day had Dada running back and forth for shopping; fruit and veg, collecting the turkeys and laying in enough bread and other iron rations for the siege that was the few days of Christmas. Maurice and Frank ferried drink, and the women put away and prepared, baked or cheered on whilst someone else did, depending on their talents.

Most of us went to Midnight Mass, and Claire too, feeling grown-up, knelt beside me in the cheery gloom of the parish church, singing 'Away In A Manger' and 'Silent Night', while I, in my secret heart, prayed and prayed for a solution, a light, even a glow at the end of the tunnel. By the time we got out it was just starting to snow. Perfect.

Back home with ham-and-stuffing sandwiches from Frank, we bowed to Claire's pleas to open tree presents.

In those early hours of Christmas Day there was much polite oohing and aahing from us, the adults, opening our books and soaps, unimaginative lot that we were! I had a really good present from Auntie though; a massive tent of a wincyette nightie for the winter which was to prove a greater boon than she ever knew.

Claire loved her bin of Christmas rubbish and with uncharacteristic restraint even saved half the presents in it till the morning. She staggered off to bed about 2.00 a.m. lulled to sleep by the sounds of us all singing round the piano, old old songs, familiar standards, gradually giving way to the big record player and Tony Bennett, Sinatra, Errol Garner, seeing us through the night.

Dada used to try to organize Christmas Day for maximum pleasure and minimum slaving, no easy matter in a household top-heavy with opinionated adults. As most of the cooking fell naturally upon Mama and him, he'd cook a huge late breakfast for everyone and then encouraged most of us to go out for a long walk and a drink while Mama and he prepared the meal and Auntie hoovered and tidied.

Frank and Maurice and Gabe and I went off, walking on the Downs that Christmas Day. It was beautiful. Crisp and clear. The snow had blanked everything into white perfection. You could see for miles over the country from Chanctonbury Ring. We dropped Claire at the stables on the way for a ride with her friends. We parked the car in Steyning and made a kind of circular tour of the countryside, aiming to finish up at the pub and then home.

I'm not a great walker normally and that day I was absolutely knackered. It was much tougher in snow. By the time we got back to the pub I felt I could hardly put one foot in front of the other. My back ached and the place was so full there were no comfy chairs left, just little stools in the middle of the bar.

Back home while wonderful smells drifted through the

house, I begged an hour's kip in exchange for any amount of dishwashing and sandwich-making later on. I felt guilty and antisocial, sneaking off. There was never the least pressure put on us but there was always a kind of understanding in those very communal family occasions that everyone joined in, nobody didn't take part. There would be subdivisions over the next few days. TV sport on Boxing Day; maybe a little group playing word games, but it was an occasion, increasingly rare, for us all to be together.

Auntie woke me about five with a cup of tea and I galvanized myself into festive humour and my red dress. I started off with a big cardigan on top of it for safety, but after an all-round check in Auntie's mirror, I went without. There was nothing to see. I was after all only three-and-a-half months pregnant.

It was a beautiful dinner. Mama's a marvellous and loving cook and as we sagged round the table, stuffed to the gills with pudding and white sauce, someone began to sing a carol and we all joined in. And then we harmonized 'God Rest Ye Merry Gentlemen' and 'Oh Little Town Of Bethlehem'.

We all sang – we sing well and love it. Claire was dragooned into a solo, like her big cousin Philip so many years before. All those volatile personalities seated round the table, peaceful, harmonious.

I still felt quite tired but not so desperate, as Gabe and I waded our way through all the dishes. It was quite therapeutic actually, sloshing my cloth through bits of turkey in the bowl. Piling the dishes into put-away groups. Thinking our own thoughts.

I made sandwiches for later, and stockpiled them in the fridge while Gabe warmed up the mince pies she'd made the day before. She's a fantastic pastry-maker, Gabe, inherited the light touch from Mama.

The remainder of the evening settled into a tranquillity. Having achieved the ultimate goal of Christmas dinner, we could now relax into that anarchic sloth that typifies the period between Christmas and New Year. The days would now be much the same; food and talk, and drink and talk, and walks on unaccustomed legs, and a gradual sinking into pleasant desultory.

On Boxing Day I went to the sea at Rustington with Dada and Gabe and Claire. He liked to go on that day. There was a little tiny café hut that served tea and scones and Dada liked to patronize anyone who was willing to open on Boxing Day. While Claire and Gabe threw pebbles into the sea, Dada said he wanted to talk to me, and I dropped back a bit.

I waited. This was it. He knew. He started to say that he didn't want to interfere in my life but did I have any immediate plans? He did. He knew. But then – no.

'Because if you don't, Paul, I can offer you six weeks' steady work. Mrs A is going on a course. I need someone till half-term.'

A variety of conflicting emotions assaulted me. Relief, disappointment, irritation, gratitude.

'Thanks a lot, Dada. Let me think about it. It's a long time and I don't want to tie myself up in case something comes up unexpectedly.'

'I know, but winter is a quiet time, isn't it, in the acting business, and I could probably sort something out if you get an audition.'

Ever reasonable, Dada. It never crossed my selfish mind that I should leap at the chance of all that regular money and maybe even give him some back to help with the rent for the flat that he was still forking out.

In the end, however, I did accept Dada's offer. I really needed money and fairly soon I was not going to be in a position to earn anything.

By 30 December, I was feeling hemmed in by family and ritual, there was nowhere to get away from everybody. I was sharing a room with Auntie, most easy of bedmates, but I wanted to let out my breath, slump, weep a bit, maybe. I fabricated an amazing New Year party and hurried back to London on the train. I would start work at Dada's school, St Andrew's, on 5 January.

It was cold when I let myself into the flat, icy cold, but peaceful, oh, so peaceful. There were a couple of bills on the floor and one or two late Christmas cards, but apart from that everything was as Gabe and I had left it. Marie was still away in Cambridge with her friends.

I moved through the rooms, switching on lamps, drawing the curtains, turning on the electric fire in my bedroom and the living-room. I went into the kitchen and put the kettle on the stove, switched on the immersion heater and started to put some food away in the larder. Mama had given me a little parcel of essentials. I wouldn't have to shop – go out even – for two or three days. I had two small loaves, some butter, cheese, four eggs, half a packet of bacon, quite a lot of turkey and ham, potatoes, carrots, sprouts, tomatoes, celery, two apples, one banana, three mince pies, Christmas cake, half a pound of tea, just over half a pint of milk in a tonic bottle and a screw of Marvel in silver foil – enough to hole up for a few days.

I made a pot of tea and left it warming on the stove while I filled a bucket with coal and set the fire in the front-room, with paper and firewood and cinders. I'm a good firemaker and soon had it roaring up the chimney, giving heat to the room. I switched on some indeterminate station on the radio and stretched out on the big brown couch, sipping my tea and watching the firelight while easy music washed over me.

It was like a huge sigh of relief being alone, with only myself to consider for a couple of days. I loved my family and hugely enjoyed their company, the conversation, the laughs, even the fights, but there was always the obligation when we were together as a group to be constantly aware of other people's feelings, of pulling my weight, smoothing potential strife sometimes; reacting, responding, taking part. Here, alone, I could be – nothing if I wanted, personalityless, voiceless, charmless, silent.

I loved that flat. It had been my home for fifteen years or so. I couldn't bear the thought of ever leaving it. But I knew Dada couldn't go on for ever keeping it going for us. We were irresponsible too, Gabe and I. We didn't pay proper attention when the rates bill came sometimes. It got shoved aside, forgotten and very often Dada was summonsed and had to pay extra. I really took a cool look at myself that night, lying by the fire. I had to face up to life, to reality. Make a proper living, keep myself. Maybe I should take a full-time teaching job, plan my life properly; become financially independent, adult and then . . . Then what? Then, have a baby. And then what? Keep the baby? How? Turn to Dada for help? And so it begins again. I fell asleep and woke to a dead fire about 3.00 a.m., chilled and melancholy.

I got up about two o'clock the next day, New Year's Eve and slumped around in my winceyette nightie, making bacon and egg and fried bread. I looked out over the snowy park as I ate, watching the people walking briskly in the winter wind. Families not always accustomed to being together, walking and chatting formally, Dads putting a guiding hand on the back of a new two-wheeler; here a puppy from the Dogs' Home, stumbling along with his people; there two brothers fighting over a kite.

Maybe I should go out, get some fresh air. That would be good for the baby, good for me. No. Hole up. Close the watertight doors. I had a bath, got dressed and started to clean the flat. It was pretty crummy. The three of us used to sporadically galvanize ourselves into action, but I hadn't felt like it much lately.

I started with the bathroom, a moderately easy option – Vim all round, chuck out dead toothpaste, soap, hair –

yuk. And finished with a liberal slurp of bleach in the lav. The kitchen presented more of a challenge. I emptied the larder of nearly everything and lit a rubbish fire in the old boiler, stuffing it with rotting veg, paper, penicillin bread. I washed all the shelves down and covered two with leftover fablon I found in a drawer. These for fresh food. I laid out my iron rations on them. I scrubbed the dresser, washed all the dishes and pans, rearranged them artistically on hooks and shelves. I scoured the cooker, washed the floor, bleached the outside lav and fell asleep for half an hour in the armchair by the boiler.

I woke about seven, and rang Worthing to wish them a happy New Year in advance as I would be out at my party. I found some clean laundry and changed my sheets. I sprayed polish on anything wood in my room, and the front-room, dusted and hoovered; lit the fire, made a tray of bread and butter, turkey and ham and Christmas cake, and collapsed in a heap on the couch to the strains of television's New Year build up.

About ten-thirty there was a knock on the door. Rattle, rattle at the letterbox. Familiar. Shit. Who was it? I pulled my dressing-gown round myself and called out, 'Who is it?'

'It's us. The Ivs. We're going to Trafalgar Square. Anybody want to come?'

'I've just got in the bath. All wet. I'm off to a party, thanks anyway.' I shouted through the door.

'OK, happy New Year.'

'Same to you. See you tomorrow.'

'See you next year! Good night.'

Gone. Thank God. Good neighbours, good friends, but not tonight.

I love New Year's Eve. New beginnings. Perhaps even more than Christmas. I love being with people I love, or even people I don't know. I love that moment when the final stroke sounds and everybody shouts and kisses and the first footers bang on the door, forgotten: 'Let us in!'

And in they come with coal and egg and salt and money and something growing.

I made a little tray of first-footing stuff. Someone could bring it in tomorrow. I put it on the balcony. Maybe one of the boys upstairs could do it for me.

I greeted 1964 in the company of Andy Stewart, that stalwart ally of the lone and friendless. I switched on the radio as well as the television just to make sure they had got it absolutely right and counted the chimes of Big Ben in stereo. I opened the balcony door and listened out for street shouts. Not many. Londoners don't seem to take New Year as seriously as we Northerners.

I'd found a bit of Cointreau in my larder blitz, and raised a glass to the New Year. I was not unhappy. I was on the edge of an abyss. God knows what 1964 would bring.

On New Year's Day I got up quite early to go to Mass. I washed and dressed and thought about going but felt increasingly reluctant to leave the flat. I opened the balcony door for fresh air; the baby should have fresh air. But I didn't want to join the people in the park, snowballing, the groups marching along the drive. I didn't want to have to face anyone, to speak to anyone at all. Maybe this is what agoraphobia's like, I thought. Maybe this is how it begins.

I made a little snowman out of drifts on the balcony, gave him cinder eyes and a carrot nose and put the little tray of first footings in his arms.

'I'll go out when he melts,' I told myself. Maybe I was a bit mad.

I shut the door, started to give myself things to do, little goals to move the day along. I took all my clothes out and laid them on the bed, picking out respectable outfits for Dada's school which would not show up my thickening waist. At first it was hopeless, nothing fitted. Then gradually, starting with the red-and-beige fluffy jumper, I managed about four outfits. The jumper was a lifesaver. It covered a multitude of sins. I could wear it with my cream Prince of Wales check skirt if I left the zip undone at the top. I unpicked the waistband of my grey circular skirt and folded it over a piece of elastic. Not bad. I ruffled through Marie's stuff and found a big, loose grey sweater. She wouldn't mind me having that. The skirt from my yellow Killarney suit was not particularly comfortable but it looked quite neat with a white blouse and my cream-and-beige cardigan. I knew Dada would be critical of how I looked, and trousers were out of the question, but all the possibilities were neat and unremarkable and – unfitted.

I washed all the jumpers and blouses and hung them on the airing rail to dry. I pressed the skirts and rubbed off any marks with a bit of petrol, and put them on the balcony to freshen in the snowy afternoon.

About four I realized I hadn't eaten all day. I started to worry about the baby not getting enough nourishment. I made a proper meal with my vegetables and ham and turkey. I noticed increasingly that each time I ate, I thought about the baby and what was good for it.

After lunch I moved through the flat, hoovering and dusting all the other bedrooms. I found only two more clean sheets, so I remade Marie's and Gabe's beds with one clean sheet each, and the other top to bottom. Better than nothing.

It was becoming colder as night came. I stopped looking for things to do and tucked up in the front-room with the television and the fire, and put Herbie Mann 'Salute to the Flute' on the radiogram. The phone rang and shocked me momentarily. I didn't want to speak, to communicate. Ring, ring, persistent. Then stopped. Then again – four rings and stop. It was family. The next time I picked it up.

'Hello, Mum.'

She wanted to know about the party.

'Wonderful.'

I found myself describing in vivid details the food, the people, the house.

'. . . beautiful house in Kensington. Sarah from school, remember Sarah?'

'Lots of her brother's friends from Cambridge were there.'

'. . . I wore my silver dress.'

'No, I wasn't cold, I took my black coat.'

'Finished about three. Paddy brought me home. Just a friend.'

'Very nice.'

'No, he didn't come in for coffee. We were too tired.'

'Just having a quiet evening tonight for a change.'

I am a good liar, it's easy.

'All right, Mum. Happy New Year to everyone. Good night and God bless.'

Alone again.

I remembered my skirts on the balcony. They were cold and stiff. Looking across the night park everything was white and still and glistening. Nobody about. I'll leave the curtains open for a while. Can't bear not to see this beauty.

The television is an intrusion. After the news I switch it off and comb the bookcase for something to suit my mood.

The Story of Mrs Murphy by Natalie Anderson Scott.

One of my all-time favourites. It's the story of an inebriate, a hopeless drunk of incredible charm who ends up losing his identity, wife, life. 'Mrs Murphy' is the drink.

'Booze is your wife. Booze, that's who you're married to.'

I don't know why I like it so much. I'm not, never have been a great lover of drink, but I suppose the wino hero came under the umbrella of tramp/hobo so beloved by Dada and I. I'd been reading it and re-reading it since

I was about fourteen. Luxuriating in the hopelessness of it. A good book to cry over.

As the night progressed, I found not only did I not want to leave the flat, I hardly wanted to leave that room. I wanted an increasingly circumscribed space for myself.

It started to freeze hard and I couldn't face the drop in temperature of my bedroom. I wanted to stay here on this couch.

I make an effort. I leave the room. Bring in blankets and pile them on the couch. Fill two hot-waterbottles. I bank the fire up high and top it with slack from the bottom of the coalhole to keep a slow burn through the night. I make a little tray of food and put a fresh pot of tea in the hearth, right up against the grate to keep warm. I read and read and read and weep, for the hobo hero and for myself and then I fall asleep.

On 2 January, I scarcely left the couch except to go to the bathroom, fill the coal scuttle and make tea. I read and drowsed in the warm room. Someone rattled on the letterbox about five, but I didn't answer. Didn't switch the lights on nor the television nor radio. I slept again and woke about 2 a.m., listened to some news, ate a bit of toast and put my head under the blankets again till morning.

And then it was over. Nothing had changed. My insurmountable problem was still with me but I was out of the dark pit, for the time being anyway. Gabe would be back tonight and Marie tomorrow. I started teaching on Tuesday. I had to gather myself, make myself cope and so I did.

By the time Gabe arrived, I had music in the frontroom, a fire in her room and an omelette in the pan.

Spring 1956

I had a strange feeling of desolation in biology yesterday.

Miss Wilson was teaching us about the brain and I was really enjoying the lesson. I hate most science but I really love biology. Then suddenly she was telling us that we only use about one tenth of the brain's capacity, and she was comparing it to an iceberg with nine tenths out of sight and she said the brain is like that; a huge part of it subconscious and we don't have access to it. She quoted a few examples of an uncommon kind which expand the brain's use — like telepathy. But told us it was not widely practised.

I felt sadder and sadder. The feeling clung to me all day. I felt a sense of loss at all the things I would never have knowledge of, all that whole part of myself locked behind a door with no key.

In bed last night I started to think of other beings — not of this earth. Of how they might have more knowledge than us; better use of their brains. Then I made up a poem about a spaceman who came to visit me. Most of it disappeared into my subconscious by morning, but this end bit stayed in my mind of when we said goodbye:

> *Love kissed my cheek.*
> *Truth clasped my hand.*
> *And then I knew of ours and his*
> *Which was the better land.*

I arrived at St Andrew's on the fifth, with seconds to spare. Dada, despite having come from Worthing, had been in his office since just after eight, and was understandably fed up that I'd cut it so fine. I would go into the classroom ill-prepared. I had a detailed plan of work from Mrs A so the children's routine would be the same but I really knew nothing about them, their strengths, weaknesses, idiosyncrasies. I had treated him like any other supply job. I'd let him down. I would make it up to him. I would make it the best six weeks' teaching I ever did.

It was a remarkable school to come into. We'd made

odd visits as children, we three girls, but to see the school from the inside was to reinforce all I had ever heard about Dada's dedication to the profession. He was one of those rare creatures who actually delight in giving children the tools for learning. Although he had been a headmaster for a good many years, at that time he was still *a teacher*, still took classes, still taught children how to read. His minute study which he shared with his secretary was always filled with little heaps of children mouthing their way through *Janet and John*. He was absolutely certain that the ability to read was the key to a magic world of independence and delight that no child should be without. He was a great champion of comics, using them as an incentive to those who found books daunting.

Although he was often urged to progress in the profession, Dada was not ambitious and eschewed grander career moves in order to remain twenty-five years Head of St Andrew's, that tiny scruffy, under-funded school. In that time he gathered round him a uniquely dedicated group of teachers, all fired with love and enthusiasm. I think he had a lasting influence on the lives of all his pupils. I still get letters from people of all ages paying tribute to his contribution to their person-alities. What most of them remember is how valuable he made them feel, how he polished their best bits and mended their mistakes. I think he knew every child who passed through his hands as well as us, his own three girls.

So after assembly, I threw myself into the classroom and tried desperately to re-create the pleasure and structure that was the hallmark of the school. I couldn't have wished for a better class. They were eights to nines, bright, enthusiastic, energetic and already very well taught.

I faithfully followed Mrs A's plan of work and tried to imbue my lessons with joy and originality, but kids can spot a fake a mile away. Thousands before me and thousands after have used the teaching profession, plundered it on the way to other things and I was no worse and probably better than many, but I was aware of the great tolerance those children showed me as I gave a pale imitation of what they were used to.

I did enjoy my time there. I was very tired all the while but I had tremendous support from all the staff who sustained me with bits of advice over cups of tea at playtime.

I was terrified that somebody would spot my condition but nobody ever did, as they smiled indulgently at my drama-student baggy jumpers.

Towards the end of six weeks, Dada gave me an afternoon off for an audition. James had put me up for a part in a Frank Norman play, *A Café Up West*, at the Theatre Royal, Stratford East.

As I left that lunch-time I walked across the playground with Miss Cullen. Dada was emerging from a manhole in the yard.

'What's he doing down there?' I said.

'Stoking the boiler. Mr O'Mahoney, the caretaker, has got a bad back. Your dad's been doing it for a couple of years.'

'He's so proud of you, you know,' she said. 'He does want you to succeed as an actress.'

He won't be. He won't be.

Unbelievably I got the part at Stratford East, being directed by Joan Littlewood. I was dazzled at the prospect of working with her. Of all the figures in the business, she came closest to my ideal of what theatre should be. I had never been much impressed by the traditional big companies. Without any real knowledge I felt the RSC was élitist and self-congratulatory, seeking to please and impress only those within the ranks of the profession, without much recourse to the taste and opinions of real people.

Joan Littlewood on the other hand seemed to have her ear to the ground and actively encouraged work from people away from the traditional nurseries of university and privilege. Frank Norman was an East End taxi-driver with a wonderful ear for dialogue and a natural sense of theatre.

I turned up for the first rehearsal in the inevitable red hairy jumper and my Killarney jeans, pinned halfway down the zip. I'd been so gobsmacked by getting the job that I hadn't really thought through whether I'd be able to do it. But it seemed it would be OK. We would rehearse for three weeks and play three and a half. I would be nearly sixteen weeks pregnant by the time I'd finished. Just OK. The part was not particularly glamorous so I could probably bluster my way through any awkward costume choices.

The atmosphere at Stratford East was wonderful. I felt as at home as I had in Killarney, but supercharged by the presence of Joan Littlewood. She was a short and unprepossessing figure in an indeterminate jumble of clothes with a witty currant-bun face.

We worked on stage almost immediately, improvising a bit and then reinforcing it with bits of scenes. A lot of my work was with Kenneth Gardinier, who played my husband and I felt an immediate rapport with him. With some actors you know that whatever ball you throw at them, they'll catch it and chuck it back. Ken was one of those.

As the first week progressed I became very aware of the difference between working at a job you can do and one you love doing. I had been marginally better paid as a teacher but the energy I could bring to this job that I really loved was markedly different from what I had to offer the children of St Andrew's.

The whole organization of Stratford East was geared to make the theatre a part of the community. There was a homey and cheap canteen which was open to the public as well as us, and the place was very well run by Gerry Raffles. There was a general air of organized informality and I began to have fantasies about getting some kind of permanent job at the Theatre Royal. Maybe as a stage-manager or in the office, and moving to the East End. Maybe an unmarried mother would be more easily tolerated in such an atmosphere. The fact that I had demonstrably no talent as a stage-manager and didn't know the first thing about office work never entered my head.

Towards the end of the week James phoned me at work. That in itself was a real buzz, made me feel like a proper actor ('Your agent's on the phone'). He'd got me a radio recording next Thursday and Friday afternoon, if Joan could give me half of Friday off. She would.

I looked forward to the weekend, relaxing, learning my lines and thanking God for this wonderful job. On Saturday I had a phone call from Eileen Murphy. Jack McKuan had a fit-up tour of *The Year of the Hiker*. He'd been let down by the juvenile and Eileen could help him out for a week or two, she'd already played the part, but then she had to do her series. Did I want to do the rest of the tour – five weeks? He'd sent off a script just in case.

I was really sad to have to turn it down. John McMahon and Joan Steynes were in the cast and I would have loved to work with them again. We nattered on for a bit and then said goodbye and good luck with our respective jobs till we meet again. She gave me the number of the first-date theatre, just in case.

On Monday morning the script of *The Year of the Hiker* arrived. I stuffed it away and went off to work.

After we'd staggered through the first half, Joan was pleased with us and started to outline in some detail how the play would progress, and what images she wanted at various points in the narrative. There was a point in one scene where I was required to appear at the top of the stairs, having got out of bed, following Ken. During rehearsals we were working on rostrums and she showed us the set and described how the stairs were fairly impressionistic, and I would be back-lit, and in sharp focus at the top of the staircase.

'I've got Jen looking for a négligé for you, something diaphanous, so we can see your shape through it.'

I stopped breathing for a second or two.

'Oh, Joan, I've always seen her in something a bit more naff than that, something quilted and floral.'

'Have you, love? Well, I'd like us to see another side of her, which is just for the bedroom. You can keep your knickers on, if you're shy.'

The rest of the day ran by me in a haze of panic. My stomach would not stand up to that kind of scrutiny, to being back-lit into sharp relief at the top of the stairs.

I didn't know what to do. I spent Monday night in sleepless torment, examining myself with and without clothes, nylon nighties draped over me and round me. I thought I looked very pregnant already. God knows what I'd be like by the end of the run. What could I do?

Towards morning I had an idea. I hunted out the Irish play. It was a good play and the juvenile was a nice enough part. More importantly there was nothing to suggest that I would have to reveal any part of my body. It was a young woman on her wedding day and she spent the whole play in a wedding dress.

Next I searched high and low for the bit of envelope on which I'd written Eileen's number. In that flat, where never a duster was raised in anger, someone had tidied it away. In despair I prayed to St Anthony, and found not Eileen's, but the number of Jack McKuan's digs that week, tucked in the script.

At 7.30 a.m. I phoned him.

'Mr Jack McKuan please.'

'Oh, he's not awake. He was very late at the theatre.'

'It's very urgent.'

'Well, he doesn't like to be disturbed.'

'It really is absolutely desperate. Tell him Pauline Collins will do the job.'

Away she went for endless hours and eventually Jack staggered to the phone, bog-eyed but delighted.

'Can you come tomorrow?'

'No, Jack, I've got a radio on Thursday and Friday. I need the cash.'

'Well, come on the Saturday night-boat, and I'll meet you in Dublin and drive you down to Mallow. We'll rehearse Sunday afternoon and hope for the best. It's not a huge part.'

We arranged that I would go to Eileen's flat in Baggot Street, have a couple of hours' kip and Jack would collect me about 1.00 p.m.

I'd get £15 a week for five weeks. Jack would send me my return ticket.

Well, that was the easy part. Now I had to face Joan and everyone else, and James.

I had some breakfast and took a cup of tea to Gabe and Marie, who were surprised but grateful.

I had to drag myself to Stratford East that day. I felt as though I was walking backwards with every step. Putting off the evil moment of having to face everybody.

I thought I should tell James first, so I had to rehearse normally from ten to eleven-thirty, and then whipped out to the public phone box in the coffee break. I listened to James' splutters of mystified disbelief while I explained that I'd got my dates mixed up and I'd already promised to do Jack's tour months ago, how it was a matter of honour. I quashed all James' offers to mediate for me with Jack McKuan; I ignored his increasing frustration as he tried to explain what I was chucking away. And what was the point of having an agent and getting myself work?

'No,' I said. 'I'll talk to Joan myself. It was my fault and I must do the explaining.'

'Well, you seem to be going your own sweet way anyway.'

I said goodbye and thank you and didn't see him again for a very long time.

Back in the theatre it was difficult to find a gap to speak to Joan, so I had to wait another agonizing hour or so till lunch-time.

I grabbed her in the dark of the theatre. I somehow felt that in the light Joan, shrewd cookie that she was, would see the lies in my eyes. I gabbled out my story, adding a little here and there to heighten my case for loyalty. I begged her forgiveness, pleaded that I was easily replaceable. She was amazed at this shock out of the blue, but I'm sure she knew that underneath my pie little story there was something more desperate. She didn't give me a hard time except momentarily.

'You're not easy to replace. That's why I chose you. But we'll manage if we must.'

I sat miserably in the canteen through lunch, saying goodbye and apologizing. I'm sure the rest of the cast thought I was mad. I was going to miss them – especially Ken. I didn't actually know how to take my leave.

Gerry Raffles did it for me as he sat down with his plate of food.

'You needn't think you're very popular here, you know.'

'No – I'm going now. Goodbye. I'm sorry.'

I never worked there again.

I was exhausted by the time I got home. One more hurdle to face. The family. I rang up and gave them the same story. They couldn't believe it. Dada said he would ring Jack McKuan. He was sure that anybody would understand what an opportunity was being lost. Mama said James could find someone else for Jack McKuan. She would ring him, and suggest that. Things were getting out of hand. I decided to bring in the big guns. I was an accomplished liar. Why not one more to still their dangerous activities?

'There's another reason I don't want to do the play . . . I have to appear naked in it.'

That shocked them into silence. Poor Mama and Dada. Was there no choice, no leeway?

'No choice, no leeway.'

'OK, then off you'd better go to Ireland.'

I felt terrible after I'd put the phone down. I was becoming more and more entrenched in a quagmire of lies.

I had a lot to do now if I was to be ready for leaving on Saturday. I had clothes to sort out, the play to learn and somehow to find a wedding dress for the play that would not make me look pregnant. I couldn't risk relying on Eileen's costume. I felt hopeless and weary and confused and alone. I went to bed and didn't wake up till Tuesday. Nineteen hours.

I washed all my biggest clothes and in the afternoon trailed round Clapham Junction and Lavender Hill looking for a wedding dress. It was a fruitless search. Everything was very nipped in at the waist. (What about all those brides who don't make it to the altar until they're seven months gone?) In the end I decided to make one and bought material and trimming at Arding & Hobbs.

That evening I sat with the script on the table in front of me and tried to sew and learn at the same time. Not an easy task. Especially as I never really progressed beyond an apron at school. Somehow I cobbled into shape an empire-line wedding dress. The basis was there by about 1.30 a.m. when I fell asleep.

I ironed and packed and did more learning on Wednesday and in the evening Marie took me through the play while I sewed a big lace bow down the front of the dress.

On Thursday morning my ticket arrived. Tiny passport to freedom. Oblivion even. In the afternoon I did part one of my radio play and acquitted myself moderately well. They were a pleasant laid-back gang but I couldn't help missing the energy of Stratford East. I went home in the evening to more learning and more sewing. I was on the worst part of the dress now, tacking on end-less rows of finicky lace. I hated the lace, the dress, myself, everything.

It was a relief to finish the play on Friday, to know another goal had been accomplished, a few more quid in the bank. I couldn't face any more of the dreaded dress. I could maybe finish it on the boat. I was all packed, more or less word perfect, and Marie made us a lovely meal to wish me on my way.

On Saturday I took a taxi to the boat-train and found myself bound once again for Ireland, a country that I love.

Summer 1956

France is wonderful. I've spent the whole summer with the le Douarins in Vannes. I was only meant to stay three weeks but I'm staying six. I love it so much. I feel completely at home here. I feel I belong here. I feel I am French. When I lost my wallet a couple of weeks ago I worried in French. Even when I had a nightmare it was in French and I woke up crying in French!

I nearly wasn't able to go. We've been very short of dough, and Mama and Dada didn't have the money for the fare and to pay the le Douarins, but then Mama got a bank loan – thank God – for £50. So everything was OK. I haven't got to pay the le Douarins for the extra three weeks. Next year, Anne-Marie will come to us, a straight swop – no money and for ever and ever I hope!

Anyway I had the fare and everything but I was very short of clothes. I had some T-shirts and a lovely pair of red-and-white striped pedal-pushers. But a big part of my holiday outfit came from Mrs Dixon downstairs; stuff that Marion had grown out of. She's given me loads of stuff, one terrific complete outfit – playsuit, shorts, blouse and skirt – all matching. Thank God for Mrs Dixon.

Going on the boat to St Malo was wonderful. Travelling alone. Mama booked me a berth and I actually met the girl I shared with on the train from London. She was Armenian – going to her penfriend in Dinan. On the boat we made friends with a French girl who had no berth so I let her share my bunk. We had a picnic and talked and I practised my French.

Next morning in St Malo I had a four-hour wait for the train to Rennes where I was meeting Anne-Marie and her mother. I sat in a café part of the time and tied my red scarf behind my ears like the French girls.

I loved the famille *le Douarin from the moment I met them. I love the way they're so organized and they have little rituals. Every morning there is* 'Bonjour Papa, Maman' *and kisses on three cheeks because this is Britanny, and every night* 'Bonsoir'.

And meals are always absolutely à l'heure, *not like our house, where you 'eat when you're hungry', says Mama, who will cook all night if necessary. Not here. Lunch at twelve-thirty, not a second later. Once Anne-Marie and I were in the town still at twelve-thirty and she ran horror-struck through the deserted streets. Everyone was* à table, *everyone in Vannes!*

I feel a tremendous sense of the past in Britanny, especially in the churches. When we go to Mass on Sunday at St Vincent Ferrier, I can smell the years in the stones. I feel I belong here. Maybe it's the Celtic thing too, in Brittany. They have lots in common with the Irish and the Welsh.

Anne-Marie and I get on incredibly well, which is amazing because we have nothing really in common in the hobbies line. She's incredibly sporty; fencing champion, tennis champion, swimming champion. I go with her for tennis lessons to M Vivet who's an Olympic coach. I have a lesson too each week. I know it's torture for me and I'm sure it is for him. Poor M Vivet with his long shorts and his knobbly brown knees.

'Regardez votre balle, mademoiselle.'

Jean-Yves, Marie Claire and Baby Jacques are the rest of the family and with Geneviève the bonne, we all spend a lot of time at their little seaside house on the Golfe du Morbihan about half an hour from Vannes.

Cariel en Séné is my idea of perfect happiness. The le Douarins have half a house. The rest belongs to Cousine Jeanne. So we all bung in the bedroom downstairs and Geneviève and Jean-Yves and Jacques sleep in the kitchen upstairs.

Everyone in the village is a cousin. This is the place where M le Douarin was born. Closest of all is the le Penru family. Xavier is the baker. He works right through the night and sometimes when we come back late from a mariage *or a fête we go in for steaming* petits pains *and eat them in the midnight road.*

There seems to be a fête somewhere nearly every week. I've never been a dancer but here it's easy. Everyone gets into a circle and you hold each other by the little finger and swing and stamp in time to the pipes – the Breton pipes are melancholic like bagpipes but a bit sweeter. They have drums too, reminds me of the old King Billy marches.

We had a tremendous time last week. We met two brothers from Paris and spent a lot of time with them. They weren't the most glamorous of Frenchmen, not like Alain Delon or Belmondo, but we managed a bit of a snog down on the beach one night. I liked them.

The sea is very particular here. It goes very far out, leaving Les Marées, *kind of wet lands, where you find shellfish and we collect some moules for dinner. I found a dead sea-horse one day. I've never seen one before. Absolutely perfect. I'll keep it.*

I rode through the sea last week. I was terrified. Xavier said I could borrow his horse, the one which pulls the delivery cart. She's called Sautrelle which means grasshopper, a misnomer if ever I heard one! She's just about alive. I rode bareback, having mounted off the wall! I was doing really well and thought I looked quite glamorous, ambling through the shallows. Then Sautrelle started to head out to sea and swim a bit. I had a hell of a job bringing her back.

''Cule, Sautrelle, 'cule.'

The one I really love here is Xavier's son, Yves. He's in the Merchant Navy. He likes me and is really kind to me but I know he just thinks of me as 'la petite Anglaise'. *Anne-Marie's little English friend.*

It's terrible that people only see the outside of you, and don't know really what you're like. When he looks at me I know what he sees. He sees a moderately good-looking, moderately intelligent, rather young-looking girl of sixteen, just sixteen! (Last week when I got drunk on champagne and did head-over-heels down the street.) He sees someone not quite as chic as Anne-Marie. How do you get chic? It's something to do with very dark navy and olivy skin and a side-to-side walk.

But he doesn't see inside me. I'm probably quite passionate but he can't see that. He doesn't know how incredibly sad I'll be to leave next week – to leave the family, Séné, la belle France; *but most of all – him. Maybe next year, when I'm seventeen he might notice me. I hope so. Patience, patience, patience.*

Ireland

There's always a fair amount of movement between England and Ireland, especially then on the sea routes, but the winter boat was very different from its summer sister. I'd paid extra for a berth and was very glad to stow away from the all-night boozers and pukers. It was an eight-berth cabin but there seemed to be only three of us in it. A very young girl who disappeared behind her curtain and never reappeared till morning, and an eager and smiling middle-aged lady whom I knew was going to find the silence hard to bear. It was still a couple of hours till we sailed so I decided to finish the dress and then try to get a full night's sleep.

I'd been laboriously oversewing for about ten minutes when she could take it no longer.

'Lovely dress.'

'Yes, not bad.'

'Getting married.'

'Yeah. Next week.' Why am I lying?

'Oh, grand.'

'It's been a bit of a rush because my fiancé's got a job in America.' I'm becoming a compulsive liar.

'Oh, isn't that great. Whereabouts?'

'Colorado.'

'Listen, will I give you a hand? I make all my children's clothes.'

I protest feebly, but then, 'Thanks a million.'

Maisie finished my terrible dress for me. In return I regaled her with tales of my family, how opposed they were to my imminent departure for the New World. I described in detail my tall red-haired fiancé, and his prowess in his field of mechanical engineering.

Around midnight I went off to the buffet to get us something to eat. I gave the silent member a knock, but answer was there none.

I came back with a feast. Soup, sandwiches, apple pie, four teas, and three mini-vodkas with tonic. We gassed till two-ish and then I begged leave to snatch four hours' sleep.

In the dawn damp of Dun Laoghaire I hugged Maisie goodbye and thanks, and got a taxi into Dublin. Eileen's flat was in Baggot Street above a greengrocer's but I'd lost the number. We trawled up and down at seven on a Sunday morning, looking for it. All shops look much the same with their shutters down. Eventually I thought I spotted it, and hopped out to ring the bell. No answer. I was sure this must be the place. I rang again and threw a stone at the window.

'Murf.'

After a couple more shouts and stones there she was, thank God, staggering out of sleep at the window.

'Jesus, what the fuck? What time is it?'

I paid the driver and she let me in.

Eileen turned all the gases on to warm the kitchen while she made tea. She'd only come back off the tour herself the night before so pickin's were a bit thin, but she found a little stale loaf and some jam. Eileen soaked the loaf in water and stuck it in the oven. In fifteen minutes we had lovely hot crusty bread.

As she shifted into wakefulness, Eileen started to tell me about the company, how they were all looking forward to seeing me, what the digs had been like. I suddenly needed to lean on somebody. She was a newish friend, but one with whom I felt a great rapport.

'Murf, I'm going to have a baby.'

It all came tumbling out as I sat in that kitchen in Baggot Street, warming myself on the gas jets. For the first time since I'd found out, I started to cry, weary, hopeless tears. Eileen was a rock, she hugged me till I'd exhausted the flow, and then put me in her bed with hot-waterbottles and hot lemon and whiskey.

I fell into a dead sleep till she woke me at twelve. Jack was picking me up at one-fifteen. From somewhere Eileen had conjured baked potatoes and bacon, and a dish of hot custard! It was still freezing in the flat and I wrapped my coat round the nightie Eileen had lent me.

After lunch I boiled a kettle and had a shivering strip wash in the icy bathroom. Murf told me to come back to her at the end of the tour, and she'd try to think up some solutions. She took me through the play and the words went OK.

'Don't worry about the moves, you can just wing it tonight.'

'Well, Jack'll rehearse me.'

'Yes, but you won't have much time. It's a seven-thirty show.'

'I'm on tonight!' I couldn't believe this. The ultimate actor's nightmare. Tonight I would be playing a longish role in a play I'd barely learned let alone rehearsed.

Jack duly arrived and I hugged Eileen goodbye and set off for Mallow which was our base for that week. I told Jack how scared I was to be shoved straight on, but he said I'd be fine and not to worry.

In the Town Hall in Mallow I was reunited with Joan and John and met Dinny O'Shea and Siobhann Ruane, his ex-wife, and Donal O'Riordan, erstwhile cashier from the Bank of Ireland, who'd taken to the boards two weeks before encouraged by an illustrious amateur career!

We went through the moves and buzzed through my scenes and I began to feel it would not be impossible.

Then Jack took me to my digs, a cold and cheerless grey house on an estate at the edge of town. A far cry from New Street.

Our first date that week was a small town about half an hour from Mallow and we were to play in a school hall. We met at the Town Hall which was to be the grand finale in Mallow and all piled into Jack's van.

When we arrived at the school, we found the stage had been constructed of school desks jammed together at one end of the hall, and a rough curtain of blankets strung across was all that separated us from the audience. There was a minute sliver of space on either side of the wings where we could wait for our entrances and exits, and a little back door on one side. Joan and Siobhann and I made-up in the girls' lavatories, which would soon be open to the public. Next time we'd do it at home.

I have no idea how I got through that night. I was crosseyed with terror, limp from exhaustion, I tottered from moment to moment, mouthing my lines like a robot. Every time I landed in the wrong spot, Joan, playing my mother, would bear down on me crying: 'Ooh, Sheelagh,' and lug me into the right place. I tripped over my wedding dress and trapped my white high heels several times in the inkwells of the desks which no one had thought to fill in. By the final curtain I was convinced Jack wouldn't have me for another night, but we all took our bows and my applause was not one iota less than anyone else's. The audience thought we were great.

As the week progressed, the acting improved considerably, and I began to enjoy my friends again, but I hated that first base. I had the worst digs ever. I was never warmer than freezing in the house. It was so cold that even in the morning my bed was still bone-chilling, the kind of cold that strikes into your soul. I slept in two nightdresses and a dressing-gown with the coat on the bed. All to no avail.

Also my landlady fed me separately from the family in a kind of solitary state, but while they all looked on. It was quite disconcerting to be shovelling down boiled bacon and cabbage, while four pairs of eyes sat round the room and watched. I used to have an awful feeling that maybe I was eating the only food in the house. Towards the end of the week, the menu became more and more limited and by Friday and Saturday I was eating eggs three times a day, boiled for breakfast, poached with mash at lunch, and fried with chips at night. I began to think I'd get eggbound. It was a blessed relief to meet the others in town for a little afternoon tea.

Our next place was marvellous. Everyone was in together in a warm, friendly guesthouse in Cahir in Tipperary. The owner was an ex-nursing sister, hospitable, outgoing and a great cook. It was surrounded by beautiful country and Joan proposed that we should not waste it but that we should walk each day in a different direction. So we did; always John and Joan and me. Sometimes the others but always us. I found it very tiring but I dared not not go. I also felt in some way it was a good thing to do for the baby. The blood was coursing through my veins and I was getting good nourishment.

One afternoon when I was resting after the route march, I was lying on my back when I felt an extraordinary sensation. A movement in my stomach like a bird fluttering upwards, trying to get off the ground. I was scared for a moment and then I realized what it was. The baby had quickened.

You were there.

1957

Unexpectedly I've got a really good new friend, Teresa Brooke.

She joined us in the Lower Sixth from a boarding-school. Everybody was a bit doubtful at first when we saw a new name on the class lists but she just slotted into L.VI Arts like an old hand.

I love her because her humour is just like Janet's and mine. She's got a tremendous sense of the ridiculous. She feels like a relation and I feel I'll go on being friends with her for ever.

The first time I went to her house and met her mother, Mrs Brooke, I realized she was the actress from Hancock's Half Hour. *Patricia Hayes. But she doesn't make you feel like an outsider and she's not grand or theatrical. I feel really comfortable with her. Sometimes she does wonderful strange things though, that make me laugh. Once I went to Evening Mass with them and Mrs Brooke sat next to me and went through her whole part with gestures and sounds. I was fascinated and hysterical!*

Teresa has a younger sister, Gemma, and an older brother, Richard, whom I adore. I remember the first time I was there, he was quite shy but now we know each other he's like a brother, best friend, soul-mate.

He's bought an old taxi and late at night a whole gang of us drives out to London Airport to sit in the viewing lounge and drink coffee till the small hours. I love watching the planes. It makes me want to travel to far-off places. I'd love to go on an aeroplane. Maybe I will one day.

Richard's working in a garage at the moment, but he really wants to be an actor. Getting to know them all, Teresa and her family, it's rekindled all my old desires to go on the stage myself.

We went to see East of Eden *last week and wanted to be in it, and desperately wanted to be actresses, wanted to work with Elia Kazan. He's directed three of my favourite films ever –* A Tree Grows in Brooklyn, On the Waterfront, *and* East of Eden.

Teresa and I have done two shows together at school. The Mikado *when I played 'Yum-Yum' and she 'Coco'; and a lovely funny nativity play called* Christmas In the Market Place, *where I played a haughty Roman lady and Teresa the gypsy leader, Joey. She's a real talent, a real comedienne.*

I really think I'd like to go to drama school. I was going to try for Oxford but I'll never make it. You have to have A level Latin for Honours English. I joined a term late, thirteen chapters of Tacitus behind, and dear old Tacitus was the death of me. I love the poets, especially Catullus, but Latin was my fifth A level. Too difficult. Dada'll be disappointed if I don't go to university, but I feel if I can't go to Oxford, I'd rather go to drama school. I'll try to break it to him gently.

Mrs Brooke took us to a theatre club during half-term, for lunch. It's called The Interval Club in Soho. I met lots of actors and actresses. I wanted to ask them all kinds of questions about how you get jobs and what you do if you're not working. I felt embarrassed about intruding on them but somehow the conversation was easy, and they brought up what I wanted to know, just offered it. I felt happy in their company. It was a lovely afternoon and Mrs Brooke says she'll take us to the BBC Club at Portland Place another time. I can't believe my luck.

We moved on to our final base, Mount Mellick, and set up camp once again, this time in a sepulchral travellers' hotel in the centre of the town. It wasn't a bad old place, warm at least, but the manager seemed terrified of overspending on the electrical front. Nothing higher than forty watts shone down from those twelve-foot ceilings and they were well concealed from view by a job lot of shades in that indeterminate pinken tone between red and rose.

Not even in the Residents' Lounge was there a drop of lowlighting. All my previous images of a fascinating group of Bohemians a bit like the Good Companions, bundling happily from cosy boarding house to gilten theatre were vanished. Buried.

A second-string tour in winter Ireland was hard slog. We'd even had the humiliation last week of a cancelled date. The amateurs ('Aah they were *very* good') had beaten us to it with a very high-class production of *Year of the Hiker*.

Still and all the company was good and the conversation great. And anyway it wasn't all gloom and doom. We had our moments of hysteria that sustained us through the dreary times.

I remember one night we were playing a particularly inadequate hall. The stage was formed from two sets of eighteen-inch rostra, piled on top of each other and surrounded by black drapes. The wings, however, reached by a little step and a hop down, were on the same level as the audience and shielded from them by a thick curtaining that didn't quite reach the ground, leaving a gap of some six inches through which we could peep at the punters' feet. If we kept towards the back they had no sight of us because there was a very short downward rake from stage to the back of the audience.

It was a cold night but everything was going fine. Full house, good response. The ladies, Joan, Siobhann and I, had a ten-minute break in the second act, while the three men had a rather touching scene, John, Dinny and Donal. Then John left them alone and exited after us.

However, this was one of the nights when there was no exit stage left so the three of us were stuck in the wing space till we next appeared.

We sat and leaned, whispering to each other, when suddenly Joan had an overwhelming urge to pee. The freezing night had put the finger on her bladder. She absolutely had to go. We searched fruitlessly for a bucket, a vase, a jam jar even! Nothing. Then Siobhann spotted a sturdy plastic wardrobe bag in the corner.

'Here,' she hissed. 'This'll do.'

She and I held it in position while Joan took the throne. When she'd finished, Siobhann, encouraged by Joan's success, absolutely had to go too. So far so good. Knowing we had a good forty minutes to the end, I began to feel anxious and went to be third in line. I was just about to get off the can or bag, when two things happened. John McMahon came off from his touching scene to be confronted by half a bare arse.

'Janey Mack, what in the name of God—' He stomped into the corner, outraged, as far away from us as he could get.

Secondly and more seriously the stalwart wardrobe bag sprang a leak, small at first in one little corner, then rapidly growing and sending an increasingly relentless yellow river downhill to the audience. We looked round frantic for something to stem the flow. A box of tissues did the trick for about ten seconds, but then was hopeless. Eventually just as it reached the curtain's edge, John, in rage and disgust, threw us his big make-up towel. Saved at the eleventh hour. He didn't speak to us for the rest of the night. I'm not surprised. We had to buy him a new make-up towel though.

In Mount Mellick I got to know Dinny and Siobhann a lot better. She was a sweet-faced, powerful actress, then about forty. Unassuming and low key until she opened her great midden of a trunk from whence she transformed herself. There was nothing she couldn't produce from it, a range of costume changes that would put Bermans in the shade, make-up, kettles, irons, stoves, food, medicine, anything.

She and Dinny O'Shea had been long separated, but remained good mates. But very different. Where she was gazelle, he was lion, huge expansive, immensely theatrical. He was a well-known figure in Ireland, a very theatrical actor, a famous and magnificent Dame, and a terrific raconteur. There was a great sweetness about him, a kindness, and I remember one night as we all sat in the gloomy Residents' Lounge, I might have fancied him a bit under other circumstances.

I remember he was sitting rubbing his hand up and down my back, I, in the eternal red fluffy jumper. I was glad of his warm touch. His arm massaged a bit round my waist.

'Oh there now,' he said, surprised. 'You're putting on a bit there. Watch the cream teas on tour, they're fatal.'

Terrified I wiggled out of his arm and tickled him round his middle-aged spread.

'Look who's talking.' Saved.

Dinny's charisma, I was soon to find, was widely appreciated. I'd been aware of a ripple of undercurrents in the company, couldn't quite put my finger on it.

I'd sometimes see Siobhann in a rage or Donal blush and giggle, big butch Kerryman that he was.

I was pretty wrapped up in my own affairs but I did have the feeling that Siobhann and Donal had become more than passing acquaintances.

What I didn't appreciate, what I'd missed, was that she'd nicked him from Dinny! Dinny was well known to be gloriously and unashamedly bi-sexual. But so was Donal, bold strap from the Bank of Ireland.

It all came to a magnificent head one night when Siobhann locked Dinny out of the hotel and he cried and sang and shouted beneath her top-floor window.

'Siobhann, I love you.'

'Let me in.'

'I still love you.' And maybe he did.

In the end it was the double-dealing Donal that got the big E from both of them. I think they both got bored with the blushing Kerry vowels.

Poor Donal, at least he didn't get pregnant.

When the tour closed I went back to Dublin to the Murf. She was a good friend, a listening ear, a source of great solace, but in the end it was down to me. Only I could make the decisions about my life and yours. She'd suggested that I might stay in Ireland as I loved it so much, have the baby in a mother and baby home. But she also warned me of the general intolerance to illegitimacy and unmarried mothers.

164

'I'm sure they're much better in London,' said Murf. 'Why don't you try that when you get back?'

It was a good idea and one in my confusion that I hadn't considered.

Eileen saw me to the night-boat. We gave each other a big hug.

'Thanks for everything, Murf. Come and stay with me when it's all over – one way or the other.'

December 1958

Life is really good in the Sixth. We have a common-room and most of us are very compatible.

Best of all a whole gang of us go out with the boys from St Paul's. Jacky, Val, Janet, Teresa and I. We have parties and go to matches (in which I feign interest) and see each other's plays and shows. Teresa's boyfriend, David Jennings, is the absolute star of St Paul's. He's wonderfully handsome and romantic and has the most beautiful singing voice. I think they really love each other – seriously. And I love my Brian.

We've been talking a lot about going 'all the way' with our boyfriends but I don't think any of us dare. In the meantime we pet and neck within an inch of our virginities.

I spent most of one night in St Paul's Sixth Form common-room. All old stones and history. It was a wildly exhilarating and nerve-racking experience. Put the kibosh on gropes though, every time we heard a noise I shot up.

Back in London I realized I really had to get moving. I couldn't conceal my pregnancy much longer, and I had to go somewhere, away from the family, quite soon.

I rang Tony and asked him to come with me to Westminster Cathedral to get some help. Having been brought up in the Church, loving nuns and trusting priests, I thought that was the place to turn to.

Having asked to see a priest, we were shown into a room and I baldly outlined my situation, while he stood and looked at us. He didn't ask us to sit down, not even then. Didn't offer consolation – why should I have expected it?

'Is this the father?' He pointed at Tony.

'Yes.'

'Yes I am,' said Tony.

'Why don't you get married?'

'Well, Father, we've thought of that, but we don't really love each other.'

'Then why did you make a child?'

'We thought we did.'

He was silent and plainly exasperated by our situation, our irresponsibility. He wrote an address and phone number on a piece of paper.

'Here – go to see them, they'll advise you further.' He opened the door. 'And pray to God to ask forgiveness for your sin.'

'Yes, Father.' Although secretly I thought it was you that I should be asking for forgiveness.

I rang the society and two days later had an interview with Miss C, who was kindness itself, not judgemental and very organized. Within the space of twenty minutes she had me booked into a mother and baby home, run by the nuns. I was to enter on 15 May and leave six weeks after you were born; about three months in all.

'And is it your plan to have the baby adopted?'

'Yes.' I hesitated. 'I think so.'

'Well, you'll have plenty of time to think about it,' she said gently. 'No need for a final decision yet.'

Her kindness caused a great welling of tears inside me and I fought to push them down.

She took details about my background and told me what the home cost – £4 10s 0d a week, all found. And how to claim benefit to pay for it.

'It's OK, I can pay, I've saved.'

'You don't need to.'

'I want to.'

I thanked her, shook hands, and said goodbye.

Paris, April 1959

I fell in love in Paris in April. So did Teresa. We were doing a very short course at the Sorbonne for our A level French. We fell in love with two of our guides, Frank and Gerard. The marvellous thing was we were not desperately in love, we were joyfully in love. Everything was more happy, more interesting, even more new because we were with the boys.

We sidestepped a lot of the official stuff and we'd go off to special places with them. We still did the Sorbonne lectures because that's important and M Tesedre was a fantastic speaker, but we elbowed all the culture.

It started on the second afternoon when we went to the Louvre. Gerard was in charge of our group and, just when he'd handed us over to the Art Guide, he looked over at me and said: 'Tu veux rester ici ou viens prendre un petit café avec moi.'

I looked at Teresa.

'Et ta petite amie.'

'On va visiter tout de suite "Vénus de Milo" et puis on viendra avec toi.'

We flew up the stairs, took a quick shufti at the armless one and then ran outside where Gerard was waiting with Frank. We knew him already.

And then everything just fell into place. Teresa and Frank instantly adored each other and Gerard and I were twin souls.

He was a curious mixture of boldness interlaced with moments of extreme shyness; Frank was much more upfront and a leader.

We did everything together, our gang of four, cafés,

167

markets, walks by the Seine; idiot things like creeping up on courting couples in the Bois de Boulogne and shouting: 'Et la morale alors.'

We were often late back to the Lycée Henri IV and we'd be throwing stones at the windows for someone to let us in.

We talked endlessly, usually in French and never wanted the week to end.

But it did. They came to see us off at the train but Gerard was in a desperate low and wouldn't say goodbye properly, just stood back with his hands in his pockets. Frank tried to compensate giving me extra hugs and kisses but it wasn't the same.

I kissed Gerard but he kept his head low. Then it was off, the train, we, hanging out of the window, waving goodbye for ever, and then Gerard lifted his head and nodded, and took one hand out of his pocket and gave a little wave. And then I knew he loved me.

When I got home to the flat, I went to put a dressing-gown on, to slump for a bit. I caught sight of myself in the wardrobe mirror. I was looking really pregnant. I couldn't stay around the family a moment longer. I'd have to go away for the next six weeks or so. Somewhere away, where nobody would know me, until it was time to go to the home.

I rang Tony and told him about the home.

'I've got to leave London now though. I can't stay till mid-May. I've got to find somewhere . . . soon.'

'What about Ireland?'

'No. Not Ireland. I'll ring you . . . will you come with me . . . ? For a while . . . if you're not working?'

A breath. 'I will if I can . . . but I'm skint, I must work.'

'OK, see ya.'

I got dressed and went to Checkleys and bought *Dalton's Weekly.* Then I went next door into the bank and asked for a current balance: £104 10s 0d. I'd saved well from the teaching, a bit from the tour and Frank had given us girls £20 each at Christmas.

I went home and stared at the *Dalton's*. I had no idea what I was looking for.

I made some tea and sat in the yellow afternoon, trying to think rationally.

1. I had to find somewhere away from London but not too inaccessible for the home.
2. It had to be as cheap as possible.
3. It had to be safe, in a safe place.

I leafed through *Dalton's* rentals in a daze – Devon, Cornwall, Gloucester, Lancs, Rutland, Somerset, West Sussex – definitely not. Wilts – no, no, no – landlocked witchy county. I wanted the sea, to be near the sea. Yes, the sea. At least I'd found some kind of direction. I would find somewhere by the sea. It would be a holiday. It would be good for my health, good for the baby, you, to have sea air. In the middle of all the dreadfulness, I began to giggle all alone there. I felt like some retired gentlewoman planning her off-peak annual holiday. I took up the paper again and began to enjoy myself. I could go anywhere. The world was my oyster. Well, anyway, *Dalton's Weekly* was my winkle.

I eventually settled upon Weston-super-Mare:

> Well-furn. flatlet. Ck. Fac. G. Floor.
> Walk to Sea. £4 wk.

It was considerably dearer than I'd envisaged but for some reason it felt the right one. I rang the number and a pleasant-voiced Mrs Palmer described it to me. She seemed very surprised that I wanted it for six weeks, but I told her I needed a rest and that my husband and I would be arriving the following Saturday. That was fine, she said, but in view of the length of stay, she would need one week's deposit. I said that would be in the next post, and thanks, and see you next week. I put the phone down.

I felt as if I was putting together some awful jigsaw puzzle, pressing the arrangements of my life into place. Now for the lies. I rang Mama.

'Hello, Mum, guess what?'

'What?'

'I've got a really lovely job. Another tour, quite a long one I think – all round the West Country – maybe further.'

'Is it a good company? Proper Equity contract?'

'Oh yes. Group of Three.'

'Who's the director?'

'Ben Hawthorne.' From God knows where I pulled a name. Actually I did know where. Ben was a well-respected actor–director whom I was later to know and love when we did Music Hall together at the Green Man, Greenwich.

But at that time I'd auditioned for him once, extremely badly. I remember it well. It was for a musical and I sang 'And This Is My Beloved' from *Kismet*. At least I tried to sing it. The song has a bit of a difficult entry three-quarters of the way through a bar after a run-up, and could I make that? I could not. Matters were not helped by the fact that Ben's little dog, scenting my anguish, started to bark each time Ben began the introduction. After six tries I gave up! So I never got that job! I did remember though, he had a company with a name something like Group of Three.

'I'm leaving in a week. Bit short notice. Someone must have dropped out. Lucky for me.' I was a consummate liar.

'Well, come and see us before you go, lovie. You haven't been down since before Ireland.'

'OK, Mum. I'll try but I've got so much to do.'

'All right, Paul, do your best.'

'Bye, Mum, see you soon.'

When I'd put the phone down I sat with paper and pen to work out my finances. The weeks in Weston were going to put a severe strain on my plans. I'd reckoned on £54 for the Home, but now with £24 rent and a minimum of, say, £3 for food and necessities each week – that would take me to £96. I still had to find my fares to Weston and the convent, and buy your layette, three nighties, a dozen nappies, three coats, three dresses, three vests, one pram suit, and two towels for you, two for myself. I didn't have enough money.

Who could I borrow from? Not Tony. He was broke. Marie and Gabe were only just managing themselves. Too dodgy to ask the family. Except – I suddenly thought – Frank! He was in Amsterdam the following week on business. I could phone him and ask for a loan – say I needed a better wardrobe for the tour. I prayed he wouldn't change his plans, that the Dutch trip was still on. I'd have to go to Worthing now to find out where he would be. I decided to go that evening, before my stomach blew up even further. I left a note for Marie and Gabe and went to Worthing, wearing my inevitable red fluffy jumper and my jeans, unzipped to the crutch.

They were delighted to see me, but observant as ever.

'You're not still wearing that bloody red jumper are you? I never see you in anything else.'

I laughed. 'I know. I've got to get some new stuff.'

We had a nice evening. I regaled them with stories of Ireland and we all chewed over the possibilities of the new job.

'I think you're on your way, Paul,' said Dada. 'You seem to be doing very well.'

I smiled, devastated by his pride in my conniving, double-dealing self.

'I thought you'd find it much harder in the beginning.'

I eventually found out where Frank was staying in Amsterdam by a series of casual manoeuvres. So – mission accomplished. Two missions.

I really had wanted to see them. I suddenly thought going down on the train, What if I died? People do die, sometimes, in childbirth. What if I died and I had not gone to see them? This way they had a good memory. They would remember me amongst them, telling stories and be glad.

What a load of shit! One too many readings of 'The Little Matchgirl', I fear.

The next day Dada left, early as usual, before I woke, and left a note: 'Good luck and get yourself another jumper! Lots of love, Dada.' And there was a fiver.

Oh Dada, so welcome – £109!

The rest of the week in London was fairly frantic.

I dragged out the faithful Revelation suitcases, big and small, setting the little one aside for your stuff. I dared not buy any baby clothes here, but I thought I might get the towels in Arding & Hobbs. There was a household sale on so they'd be cheaper, hopefully.

I started my packing with something to come home in, all those months ahead – my navy blue Chanel suit. When I say Chanel, I speak figuratively! Chanel-type! It would be summer then, so blouses, summer skirts – not too much. Big nightie, dressing-gown. I wished I had a better one. Couple of cardigans.

I had absolutely nothing to wear during those last few weeks of pregnancy. I was bursting out of all my skirts. They'd have to do for another couple of weeks. What then? Maternity smocks?

I rang Tony to tell him all my news and we met for a coffee in Bayswater, near where he lived. He said he'd come with me to Weston for a week or two at least, and I was glad. It was a bright afternoon and we walked through the park, sat by the Serpentine and thought our thoughts. After a bit he put forward the suggestion that his mother might bring you up. He himself had been raised by his grandmother in Ireland until his mother married his stepfather. Intransigent as ever, I blanked this idea out, once again denying Tony an opinion.

He kept me company to Knightsbridge and then we went our separate ways. I was on my way to the 137 home when I saw Harrods across the road. I hadn't been there since my brief period of employment after leaving drama school. I thought I'd have a look around. It was like being wrapped in a cashmere blanket. Everything was clean and quiet and orderly and beautiful.

I went straight to the baby department and looked at the tasteful displays of French and Italian couture for *bébé* and *bambino*. I stroked the lace and broderie anglaise, and felt the soft, soft woollens. I wanted to buy something for you here. Everything was outrageously expensive. Then I saw exactly what I wanted, a pram suit in the softest wool and the softest yellow imaginable. That was the one. I looked at the ticket – £4 15s 0d. Hopeless. I looked further along the bar and found a lovely white one. Still £3 10s 0d but better. I had no money on me anyway. I put them back, wrote a brief description on a bit of paper and put it in my bag.

I wandered round the store for another half an hour or so, ending up near the Tea Room.

AFTERNOON TEA. SANDWICHES, SCONES AND FANCIES: 2s 6d.

It looked lovely. Then I thought, No, that's a bit of a pram suit!

I went home and made myself hot-buttered toast and rich tea biscuits. Not quite in the same league, but welcome none the less!

There was an inevitability now about my progress that cheered me up. My problems were still there but at least my life was mapped out for the next four and a half months.

The security of it made me a bit bold, and one

afternoon, having got my bargain towels in Ardings' 'Special Event' I was on my way home via Lavender Hill, when I saw a little shop. In the window was a navy blue pinafore dress worn with a pink blouse. It looked neat and smart. Hanging from the model's languid arm was a sign: FOR THE LADY IN WAITING. It was a maternity dress! I had a quick look round. Nobody I knew so I went in and asked to see the dress.

'For yourself, duck?'

'My cousin. But she's about my size, a bit bigger maybe.'

'Here's a ten. Bring it back if it doesn't fit. 22s 6d.'

I rushed home and tried it on. It felt wonderful for once not to have anything tight round my stomach. I looked in the mirror. I looked solid and mundane. I tried it with all my blouses and found three looked quite nice – a white one, a blue striped and a funny, shiny-pink, silky thing. At least I looked respectable, and it provided an instant maternity wardrobe for a modest price.

The bag was still lying around when Gabe came in.

'What's this? What've you bought?'

'Just a pinafore dress.'

She held it up.

I held my breath.

'Bit shapeless isn't it?'

'A-line.'

'Oh. Want a cup of tea?'

'Yep, thanks.' Phew!

On Friday I withdrew all my money from the bank in large notes, ready to put in the Post Office at Weston-super-Mare.

I'd arranged to meet Tony the next day, Saturday, at Paddington by the platform in time for the twelve thirty-eight. So I was a bit thrown when Maurice said he'd drive me to the station. Grateful but thrown. I phoned Tony and hissed at him to meet me on the train instead, told

174

him to go right up the front, in case Maurice saw him.

To my terror Maurice carried my cases right on to the train and through the coaches. It was full so he kept on walking till we were almost in the middle. Suddenly at the end of the open carriage, I saw Tony's anxious face.

'Don't worry, Mau,' I said, desperate. 'Here's fine. There's a seat.' One left in a four.

'Let's try and find a bit more space.'

'No, this is fine.' Please go. 'Near the buffet.'

'OK.' Up go the cases.

'Thanks a lot, Mau.' I give him a kiss, truly grateful.

'Good luck – here,' feeling in his pocket, 'get yourself a nice lunch on the train.' And he gave me two pounds.

'Oh Mau, thanks.' I wave goodbye.

Then when the train pulled out, I went along to Tony and gave him a hard time for the heart attack he nearly gave me.

'Come on,' I thumped him. 'Let's get something from the buffet.' I held up the two pounds. 'I'm rich.'

1960

So we threw our berets over Hammersmith Bridge and cried and took deep breaths of excitement because our schooldays were forever over and life was just beginning.

And we all went our ways. Teresa to the Guildhall, Janet to Exeter, and me to the Central School of Speech and Drama, full of anticipation, and now here I am. And it's a big disappointment. My own fault. I took the teaching course. Faute de mieux, *the only way I could get a grant. It was a mistake. My heart is not in it and it's very frustrating not to be doing what I really want.*

I asked for a transfer to the acting course but they turned me down. Don't think I've got what it takes. Never mind.

I'll get my head down, get the certificate and plough on from there.

Meanwhile the social life is great and in Marie McGaughey, who shares the flat with me, I have a really kindred spirit.

I will try at the end of my three years to get into the business. It'll be hard because the teachers don't have public shows, don't get seen by agents. But I'll write everywhere and try to get auditions. Give myself maybe five years to make it or break it. But I will try.

Six Weeks In Another Town

It wasn't very far from the station to Bangor Road. We walked through the clean greystone streets, smelling the different air, the sea scent on the wind. I found myself breathing very deeply, very relaxed, more calm than I had been for months. Even though Tony had told me on the train that he was not going to be able to stay, I felt I was going to be all right here.

'I've got a bit of bad news for you.' He'd moved his cup round and round in his beautiful hands.

'What?' I, sharp and guarded.

'I've got a job.' Sometimes when he was nervous, he stammered the smallest bit. 'I can't stay with you. Just tonight.'

'Oh.' I cold and ungiving, staring out of the rattling window. I should have been glad he'd got a job but somehow I took it as a personal affront.

I don't know now why I gave him such a hard time, why I used him. I wanted his support but not his self. Poor Tony. I'm sure half the time in his dealings with me, he didn't know whether he was on his arse or his elbow!

Anyway, now I was here it didn't matter. I felt safe already. I'd be OK.

Mrs Palmer showed us into the flatlet, a large sunny room on the street. It was comfortably furnished with a big low double bed, two good armchairs, table and a little double-unit kitchen bar – sink, stove and cupboards. The bathroom was up one flight of stairs and the room was Yale-locked for privacy.

'I got your bit of shopping in, Mrs Rohr.'

I turned surprised, I'd forgotten I'd given our names as Mr and Mrs Rohr, to compound the image of this charming young couple taking the cure.

'Oh, thanks a lot, Mrs Palmer.'

Tea, milk, butter, bread, bacon and eggs. I gave her some money and she left us to unpack.

'Come on, let's leave this. Come for a walk.' I wanted to mend my mood with Tony. Let us part on better terms.

We found our way to the sea front easily. It's funny in coastal towns, there's always a kind of pattern that leads you in the right direction. Something to do with the light and the way the backs of the buildings change as you get one or two streets away from the front – all pipes and fire escapes. Boarding houses, private hotels, and the Victorian arcades and gift shops frame your view, and guide you to the promenade. Esplanade in this case. It was a biggish sea front in two stages, park and bandstand, then the prom itself.

'It's lovely here, I'm going to be fine.' I put my arm through Tony's as we took our little constitutional up and down the prom.

'I'll really try to get down a couple of times.' I could see he was glad the diplomatic relations were once more resumed.

'I know you will. Thanks.' But after all he really owed me nothing. He'd offered me everything. Himself. And I'd said no. He could do no more. He really owed me nothing at all.

We went for fish and chips, seaside cod and four. Lovely. And ate them overlooking the sea, while a little evening wind blew up.

Afterwards in a small pub with mullioned windows and brass horseshoes, I asked if I could send letters to him later on in St Andrews, where he had joined the Rep, so he could forward them to the family. Sure, I could.

We slept together that night for the first time in

178

months – comfortable in non-sexual ease. It was good to feel someone warm beside me and a peaceful valedictory to a loving friendship.

We had a late boarding-house breakfast the next day, borrowing a bit of lard and two tomatoes from Mrs Palmer, and then I saw Tony off on the early afternoon train. I felt curiously detached as I stood on the platform, watching his loyal hand waving until the train was out of sight and he could decently terminate this obligation, and sink into the seat and oblivion. I felt as if I was in some curious continental film, all black and white and no pace at all.

I went back to Bangor Road and looked forward to the prospect in front of me. Six weeks in another town. I remember there was a film called that once. Kirk Douglas, or was it Two? Anyway this man finds himself unexpectedly in a strange small town and proceeds to enter into its spirit in a big way. Love affairs and such. I didn't envisage my scenario taking quite such a turn, but I would try to use the time well.

I sat in my brown armchair, listening to the radio and tried to work out my priorities:

1. Eat properly.

I had to work out a good diet. I was quite tired and thought I might be short of iron, so liver at least twice a week and greens every day. Iron for the baby.

2. Buy clothes for the baby.

I hadn't a stitch yet to put on you.

3. Be very careful of my personal safety.

Only three people in the world knew where I was. I would not go out at night after dark. I could disappear and no one would be any the wiser. Also I needed some more sensible shoes. I was still clacking around in stilettos. They were very tiring and I'd already twisted my foot a couple of times.

4. Find some kind of explanation for Mrs Palmer why Tony wasn't staying.

5.   Try to enjoy myself.

I'd read babies picked up all the vibes from their mothers, and so far you'd had a bellyful of misery, so I'd try to be a bit more peaceful.

Scrambled egg on toast for supper that night. Eggs twice in one day, hardly the rich and varied diet I was planning. Never mind, *bambino*. Start afresh tomorrow. Monday is a new day. Good night.

After breakfast the next day I set off to get to know the town better, help me shape the days.

I started by depositing all my money except food money in the Post Office. I would draw out what I needed every Friday: £4 for rent, £3 for food and £2 towards your clothes. I decided if I kept to a very strict budget, I would be less likely to spend on unnecessary things.

On leaving the Post Office I spotted a rare little pleasure. A small but very well-stocked library in the back of the newsagents where I bought a paper. For one shilling a week you could borrow an unlimited amount of books so long as they were returned within the week. Paradise. I joined on the spot and picked three.

I walked all along the esplanade, looking at the municipal notice boards telling us of delights to come. Flower Festival. Not quite up my alley. Crowning of the May Queen. Should I enter for that? Naa, I'd only be beaten again by another ringlet-haired beauty. Band Concerts. I love brass bands. Tue/Thur/Sat 3.00 p.m. till 31 May, then daily. That would be something to do, free. Memories of childhood in Vale Park.

I was feeling quite hungry. The newsagent–library had a little coffee area on one side, so I walked back and had a creamy coffee and an almond tart. Mustn't do that too often, not the tart, anyway.

Just five minutes from Bangor Road was a really good small parade of shops, everything I could need. So I stocked up as carefully as I could, but forgot the old maxim that you shouldn't shop on an empty stomach. I spent a fortune, nearly a week's money. I'd have to be much more careful, especially as I had nowhere to really store food, no larder.

Still we went home to a great lunch, you and I. Liver and bacon, potatoes and the first of many yards of spring greens I was to consume. It's a wonder you didn't come out green!

I slept that afternoon, exhausted by my labours and didn't wake till six. I'll have to watch that. Use the days, sleep the nights.

I went in to see Mrs Palmer later on to offer her some kind of explanation for Tony's absence. I told her he was an actor and had suddenly got a job.

'Do you work too, Mrs Rohr?'

'Oh, I'm an actress too.' Damn, I wished I hadn't said that. Still it might explain any letters that came for Pauline Collins. 'I work in my single name.'

I didn't talk about being pregnant. I was still wearing the red fluffy, and I don't think she noticed. She suggested I might like to hire a television – five shillings a week. It'd be company, a good idea.

I put myself to bed that night with cocoa, the beginning of a ritual to get the milk into me. I felt quaint and old-fashioned and organized.

By Friday I'd made contact with Frank in Amsterdam begging a loan of £100, which he agreed to without a murmur. Thanks, Frank. I asked him to send the cheque to Marie, because the tour was moving on and I didn't yet have an address. I thanked God as I put the phone down. It had started to rain a bit, so I stayed in the telephone booth, and tried Marie. No reply. It was going to be difficult to get hold of her in the daytime, maybe a letter would be quicker.

I went to the coffee shop and bought some Basildon Bond and had a coffee while I wrote to Marie, asking her to send the cheque on. I felt wealthy beyond the dreams of avarice with that extra £100. Suddenly I had a thought. I scruffled through my bag and found the bits of information about the beautiful yellow pram suit in Harrods. I would buy it! I described it in the letter and asked Marie to buy it, or if that had gone, the white one. I stopped at the Post Office and bought a postal order to send with the letter.

I went home to lamb chops but found them too high to eat, had to settle for cheese on toast. Mrs Palmer's dog thought he'd died and gone to heaven. From now on I would shop daily.

My days settled into an orderly shape.

I would get up about nine and make tea and a moderate breakfast of fruit and toast or cereal, and listen to the news and morning music as I washed up and tidied the room so it would be nice to come back to.

Then I'd bath and dress, choosing from my extensive wardrobe of A or B, and around ten-thirty I'd begin to stroll purposefully to the sea front. I was tremendously lucky during those six weeks. On the whole the weather was magnificent. I'd walk the full length of the prom, taking a little rest here and there in a shelter, meeting the regulars, exchanging a few words – very few. Never 'intruding on each other's personalities'.

'Lovely again, isn't it?'

'Lovely. Don't like the look of that cloud, though.'

'Still, the little breeze is very nice. Very refreshing.'

'Well, off I go, best foot forward.'

Meaningless. No, not meaningless. It did have purpose. It said – I'm here. Not there with you, but here. Not too far away. If it should be necessary, but I hope it won't.

Around midday I'd find myself in the coffee shop, having bought my paper and chosen my books. I was reading a tremendous amount, nobody got better value from that one shilling a week than I did.

'Then I'd saunter slowly home, stopping at the shops

to choose our lunch; fresh white fish, lean steak. Sometimes a little row of cutlets, and always the inevitable spring greens. And I kept the fruit bowl filled with good but not exotic fruit.

I used to sometimes think I would make a model pensioner, eating sensibly, moulding my days into mini-purposes. I'd be a role model for my peer group.

Then home to a late lunch and a little rest, and a long quiet evening.

Some days when it was particularly bright and uplifting, I'd take sandwiches and tea in my thermos and stay out all day, sitting in a deckchair, listening to the band, or stretched out on a bench, reading by the sea.

Towards the end of the second week, I gave in and wore my lady-in-waiting pinafore dress. Bliss. The stilettos looked ridiculous and I found a lovely and comfortable pair of red low-heeled shoes. I also bought a red maternity dress exactly the same colour as the shoes. I thought it would do for best. For best! What best? Where was I going? I think the arrival of Frank's cheque had gone to my head. Still, it was a change from the workman-like pinafore, and I felt quite smart in it. I wore it to the band concerts, and church on Sunday.

I also wore it to the doctor. I became concerned that I'd had no kind of check-up for months so I went to see a doctor privately. I didn't lie to him at all, I don't know why. He examined me and found me absolutely fine, but he was concerned about me. Where was I going? Who was supporting me? I only saw him twice but I remember his kind face vividly, as I fended off his offers of help, and said I was fine and all organized.

I went home and cried a bit that night. Too much kindness makes me cry.

I did lie to Mrs Palmer though. When I started featuring the maternity wear, she seemed surprised and asked when it was due.

'August,' said I.

I explained that we'd been living with my mother-in-law but it was all a strain on my nerves, and now I'd be going back to a new flat of our own. She may have been a little nervous that she was going to be lumbered with a complete family in her holiday accommodation. I re-assured her.

I planned a day each week to go to another town and send a postcard or letter from there to the family. Bristol, Minehead, Taunton.

I would walk the streets and choose an address: 15 Summerlane Road, 270b Arnold Avenue, 7 Everleigh Road.

I was worried that this fictional tour was in a bit of a small area, but it was the longest journey I could make in a day. I spoke too of our imminent departure for the Scottish leg of the tour.

I quite enjoyed those days. It made a change from the matronly progress of my normal routine and gave me an opportunity to buy clothes for you that were special and chosen after seeing lots of stuff.

I bought two of your lawn dresses in Minehead – all they had, and a third, one size bigger but exactly the same, came from Bristol.

In Weston I'd seen nappies on sale, slightly imperfect, but I was worried that they might be bitty and uncomfortable, so I bought full-price ones from a big department store in Bristol. Unbelievable, aren't I?

I remembered Claire having very soft nighties, 'nuns' veiling' Mama had called them, so I hunted high and low till I found those.

When I had everything complete, I bought a wicker picnic basket and padded and lined it with satin to make a little special suitcase for your stuff.

A parcel arrived one day from Marie, and in it not only the beautiful yellow woollen suit, but also the white one. That was her present to you. I was thrilled.

Looking back now over that period it was an

extraordinary time. Apart from the odd chat with Mrs Palmer who was delightful but often out, I spoke to no one on a personal level. My dealings with other human beings were all in a very superficial vein.

'Morning – lovely – half a pound of spring greens?'

'Can I help you, madam?'

'No steak today, what about a nice bit of best mince?'

'How's that little bun coming along. I bet somebody's hubby's proud.'

Even in the library where I spent a lot of time, what with the books and the coffees, everything was pleasant and impersonal.

'That's a good one. Lovely ending.'

'More coffee, dear? Tempt you to a bit of Battenberg?'

I never even knew her name, the pink-cardiganed one with the comfortable hips. I wonder if she noticed when I was gone.

Not that I minded, I'm good on my own. I like the peace, the choices uncomplicated by other people's desire. I have ample resources, mental and spiritual and I had you.

I began talking to you in Weston. Describing the days, the clothes, how I was feeling. I don't mean deep heavy feelings, I was trying to keep off those for a time, keep the gloom away. But small things, odd things that made me laugh and telling you about those transient moments of elation that come unbidden when a wind blows or the day breaks in a certain way, or a bird rocks his whole self with a song.

A couple of days before I left for the home something happened that absolutely broke me up.

As you know, the bathroom was one floor up and most nights I had to make at least one, if not two, trips during the small hours. I would totter out of bed, put the snick on the Yale lock, lumber to the loo and return, all without really waking up.

Well, very early one morning I woke about five, staggered up the stairs and back down again. I pushed the door and found it was locked. I don't know what happened, maybe I forgot, maybe I didn't do it properly but there I was at five in the morning, shut out of my room while the family slept in the nether regions.

I cursed, sat on the stairs and cursed. I'd have to wait until Mrs Palmer woke up.

Then I had a sudden moment of inspiration. The windows, I often left the windows open, maybe it wasn't locked.

I opened the front door and put the bolt out, making very sure that it didn't slam on me. Then I stood for a moment looking down the silent morning. I stepped over the low wall and stood in the little flower bed below the windows, and pushed first one, then another. No give, no luck. I was sure one wasn't bolted. I looked about for some leverage and found a bit of slate and shoved it into the bottom of the window, while I pushed up. Success! Thank God. I pushed it as far as I could and then attempted to climb in. It was quite high set, the sill, well above my crutch level. I put my hands on the window ledge, and started to try to reach a sitting position by dint of little hops and heave-ups. No good. I'm not lithe at the best of times and seven-and-a-half months gone, I was almost a non-starter. Eventually, however, with a supreme heave, and a leg up from a bit of rock, I managed to straddle the sill.

So there I was, half-dead with sleep, my winceyette nightie up round my ears, riding the window sill like some dreadful Thelwell schoolgirl.

'Morning, luv.'

Oh God. The milkman strides towards me, plonks down his bottles and strides back to his float. I die a thousand deaths and front it out, smiling maniacally.

'Morning,' and slowly heave myself out of sight and into oblivion.

I hardly dared go out that day. Every now and then it would come over me, and I'd shake with hysterical laughter. Had to watch it in public or I'd be carted off by the men in white coats.

I've got a job. I can't believe it. I left Central with my teaching certificate and not much hope of ever breaking into the business. But here I am. I have.

I got temporary work at Harrods, and as a wine waitress at West London Air Terminal. I served Paul Tortelier – bored the poor man to death. I'd written everywhere with very little result. Then came a call from Windsor for a general audition.

I performed for Joan Riley one fine and sunny day. She was very friendly and encouraging. I did a couple of pieces and she seemed pleased but not bowled over by my talent. I thanked her and left. As I went down the stairs I passed a very beautiful dark-skinned, dark-haired girl with an amazing cleavage. She looked nervous.

'What's she like?'

'Lovely,' I said. 'She's a very warm lady, you'll be OK. Good luck.'

'Thanks.' She went on her way and I on mine. Little ships passing. Little moments.

A few weeks later I had a phone call from Joan Riley. My heart sang.

'If you're as I remember you,' she said, 'I'd like you to play an Arabian maidservant in my next production, Gazelle in Park Lane.'

My heart sank.

'It's not me,' I said. 'You don't want me. It was the next girl. The girl after me. She looked very foreign. She's the one you want.'

Joan laughed. 'It's not your looks, it's your comedy I

187

want. *Come down and see me tomorrow. But I'm sure it's you I want.*' And it was.

I'm with a wonderful company: Angela Brown, Peter Grey, Daphne Newton and Barry Shawzin.

Joan's a marvellous director and everyone is incredibly kind and helpful. Peter and Daphne, who are married, live in Battersea, and often give me a lift home. Or if not them, Barry Shawzin does. He's a rare character, he's huge and domineering but I really like him.

Also he's done something wonderful for me. He's got me an agent. Actually he's forced me upon his agent, poor man. You don't say no to Barry.

James Sharkey is with the Al Parker Agency, one of the biggest. I really have had the most incredible luck.

He's very handsome and charming, used to be an actor. I hope he'll grow to like me because I'm good, not just because Barry brought me to him. I feel at the moment a bit as if he's been dragooned into accepting me. Anyway only time will tell.

I love being in a company. I went out with one of the ASMs last week, nearly lost my virginity but he kept his socks on. Couldn't stop laughing. Nice boy though.

Meanwhile I absolutely love performing each night. I love that feeling of being tied to the audience with an invisible thread, pulling each other gently closer. I wish it could go on for ever.

But it won't. Five more shows, and I'm on my own again. What next?

The Convent

On 15 May, I left Bangor Road with some sadness. I'd been curiously at peace in my small world. Still guarded against discovery but less so because I was unknown and solitary, never close to anyone, so less people to lie to, less wearing.

I ordered a taxi in time for the London express thus avoiding any more unnecessary explanations to Mrs Palmer, and hung around for half an hour for the local train to Bristol. It was to be a tedious and circuitous route to the convent. Change at Bristol, change at Salisbury. I was not travelling light. Two suitcases, holdall, plastic bag, picnic basket and handbag. The Bristol switch wasn't too bad. A woman almost as old as Mama took the big case from me and humped it over to the other platform, ordering a passing youth to sling my cases on the luggage rack.

The train was empty and peaceful as it rattled through the unknown countryside. No buffet though. I was glad I'd brought some sandwiches and my thermos.

Salisbury was a nightmare. I was galloping about on the seats, trying to reach my cases, throwing them down, pushing them out on to the platform. My next train seemed to be miles away, no porters, no good Samaritans. In the end I transferred my goods, cursing, up and down two flights of stairs in two journeys, roasting with rage in my terrible black-and-grey speckled coat. Why couldn't I be like Eileen Murphy – a one-bag person? God knows I was a one-dress person – well, two anyway. What was all the rest of this extraneous litter? I swore in a future life I would never take more than one bag. (I never do now. Queen of the hand luggage, that's me.)

I filled a carriage with my cases and bags, putting them on the seats and between them. No more antics with luggage racks. Let anybody dare approach me. No one did.

Exhausted I rooted for the thermos. Yuk, terrible, brackish, awful old tea.

'Lunch, first sitting, fifteen minutes to lunch.'

'Yes please.' I took a ticket. What the hell, I needed a little luxury, a little foolish frittering.

I felt old and dirty and awful. I opened my cases and took out the red dress, my best dress. I knew it was a good buy. I went to the lavatory, washed completely, a strip wash, rolling from side to side, put on the red dress and re-did my hair till it was stiff with pins and backcombed to new undreamt of heights.

Then I went into the dining-car like Lady Never Shit, ordering the best lunch and a glass of wine, while the train carried me to my next unknown destination.

I arrived at the convent in the middle of the afternoon.

As I walked up the path from the gate, carrying the bigger of my two cases, I saw a couple of tramps sitting outside a door to the side, eating the remains of a meal. I rang the bell.

There's always a kind of delay in a convent bell between the ringing and the answering as if the nuns have to be brought back from some distant, sweeter land to deal with this world. I pictured a black-robed figure rustling along a painted cloister (much like Hammersmith), dragged from prayer to deal with a lost one.

Wrong. The door was opened by a young, smiling nun, full of energy and joy, sensibly dressed in white with an apron and cuffs rolled up to the elbows.

'Now then – you must be Pauline – come on in, you're

welcome. Don't lift that heavy case. Ah, you've another one there by the gate. I'll get one of the mothers to bring that up for you. Come on with me now and I'll show you your room.'

I followed her through a hallway and across a large day-room with couches, chairs and a TV. Everywhere I looked there were girls.

A weary Italianate beauty passed us.

'This is Estelle. She's just had a beautiful big boy.'

'Ten pounds,' said Estelle, with a Mona Lisa smile. 'Sister, he was still hungry after the two o'clock feed.'

'I'll have a look at him in a minute,' said Sister Theresa. 'He might need a bit extra, big fellow that he is.'

'She's only fifteen,' said Sister as we moved away.

We moved on upstairs and Sister Theresa showed me the bathrooms. They were oversized, each accommodating four baths, divided from each other by partitions and door. Private yet sociable.

'Use them any time but don't lock the doors in case you feel unwell.'

She showed me a couple of small dormitories for four or six, and then took me into a twin-bedded room, simple but beautiful and peaceful.

'There's just you and Jo in here. She's a teacher so you should get along fine. You must be tired now, so unpack a bit and have a rest, and I'll get someone to bring you a cup of tea. You'll be happy here, you're safe.'

Closing the door behind her, she left to sort out Estelle's big hungry boy.

Suddenly, I felt not desperate, not ashamed, not self-loathing. I felt like a human being again.

The moment Jo appeared round the door with tea, I knew she and I would be friends. She was a domestic science teacher from Oldham. Tall, humorous, she wore the most amazing eye make-up, false eyelashes, shadow and meticulously drawn lines. Every evening she put her hair in rollers, re-created her face and slept flat on her back so as not to disturb her work.

It was strange how we all seemed to hang on to some little glamorous ritual as we rolled round the home in our ill-assorted maternity clothes. Elizabeth had long perfect nails like talons, and a lipstick to match every nail colour. Dawn who was very young, had the most amazing range of baby doll nighties. Her mother visited her often to top up the wardrobe. It was, of course, the ideal shape for maternity wear though Sister Theresa encouraged her to wear a skirt with it as often as possible!

And I continued to put my hair up every morning in the old complex way. I used to laugh at my mother whose hairstyle was (and still is) a hugely complicated network of sections, plaited and curled like the White Queen in *Alice*, now I was doing the same myself.

When I arrived at the convent, it was home to about two dozen girls, some of whom had already had their babies, who were called 'the mothers' and the rest of us, still waiting, 'the antenatals'.

The mother and baby home was attached to a community of about ten nuns, who slept and worked in their cloister, apart from Sisters Theresa and Frances who had rooms in our part of the building.

The Sisters of Nazareth Houses have a tradition of working amongst those sections of the community who most need them. They run hospices, nurseries and hostels for homeless people.

As well as looking after us girls, this community also ran a children's nursery and fed a nucleus of about six gentlemen of the road, at the kitchen door every day.

The tramps got their dinner, three courses on plates, sitting on the steps by the kitchen door, followed by tea. About a month after I'd arrived, there was a new helper to Sister Ignatious who was the chef. I noticed the 'boys' were left hopelessly waiting till well gone two-thirty before anything appeared and then with scant finesse,

Josie would thump down everything at once – tea, soup, dinner, pudding, most of it cold by then.

After a few days I went in to see her. She was washing up.

'Josie,' said I in a friendly fashion, 'you probably don't know but the fellows have their food as soon as we've finished ours, otherwise it gets a bit stewed and cold.'

'Fuck off,' said she. Ah well.

I shared with my father an admiration for those who cast aside all material trappings to wander the roads unburdened by jobs or possessions. Dada loved all things hobo. *Autobiography of a Super-Tramp* and *On the Road* were among his and my best reads.

No tramp was safe from his bounty. He would go out of his way to give five bob or a ten-shilling note to anybody raggedy, often pursuing them over long distances to hand over cash.

Two instances stick out.

Once in the local shop, seeing a thinly clad old soul wavering between 2oz butter or 2oz sugar, he slipped ten bob in her hand and left the shop. He'd only walked a few yards when a piercing shriek stopped him.

'Oih, you. What's your bleedin' game?'

Another time not long after, having moved to the coast, he spotted a shabby figure in sandals and a thin raincoat plodding towards the Downs, stick in hand and a haversack on his back. Ten-bob note at the ready, he pressed it discreetly into the man's hand.

'There you are, old fellow, get yourself something to eat.'

The man stopped marching and stared at Dada.

'I beg your pardon?' Well-educated voice.

Fallen on hard times, thought Dada. 'Have a good hot meal. It's cold today.'

The man's eyes blazed for a moment then cooled as he replied: 'It's frightfully decent of you, old chap, but I only live there,' pointing down the road to a magnificent detached Tudor house, 'I'm just out for a quiet stroll.' And marched huffily away.

Oh the embarrassment.

My parents' grand plan for retirement was to hire a motor home and drive slowly across America – the closest Dada would have been to following in the steps of his idols. He never made it. He died of lung cancer two years after he retired.

Two nuns out of the community took care of all our needs, Theresa and Frances, both nurses and midwives. They monitored our health, delivered our babies, guided us in the feeding and care of them and sent us gently on our ways after three months.

They were the perfect complement to each other. Sister Theresa was tall, outgoing and cheerful. She had an incredible rapport with the babies and adored them all regardless. She taught us to be mothers wholeheartedly for six weeks for the mutual benefit of ourselves and our children.

Sister Frances was tiny and quiet and without ever forcing her opinion was an unbiased ear, a sounding board, a counsellor and comforter.

All the work was done by us on a rota basis so nobody ended up shackled to some hated job for ever. Cooking under the kitchen sister's supervision; cleaning; laundry; preparations of supplementary bottles for the babies; helping in the nurseries. Everybody did something. Antenatals didn't do heavy lifting and new mothers had seven days free of work.

I started off cleaning the sitting-room/dining-room, and later in the milk kitchen. I was glad of the occupation while I waited for you to be born. As antenatals we worked only in the mornings and were free to do as we liked for the rest of the day. It was a bit like being at a girls' boarding-school or how I imagined one would be, never having experienced it. There was gossip and scandal, hints that one girl's baby had been fathered by a very close relative. But most of all there was mutual support and kindness.

We came from many different backgrounds. Maria Isabella was an Italian countess, ruined for marriage now that she had borne an illegitimate son, and was no longer a virgin. The day she left to give her baby for adoption, I had a more than usually heavy feeling for her. She seemed like a shell masquerading as a person. I felt in her a terrible and final despair.

One of my favourites among the girls was Molly from Belfast. She had a face like a smiling moon, strong glasses and a strange rolling gait. She had been taken for a ride in a big way by a man whom she met while working as a domestic in Newbury. She'd met him at a fairground, slept with him once or twice in a field, and given him her £200 savings to put as a deposit on a caravan now they were 'engaged'. He had also systematically stripped her of everything she possessed, her clothes, radio, hair-dryer, luggage, anything that wasn't nailed down. She couldn't understand why he'd disappeared so swiftly from her life. She had the address of a caravan site in Newbury and was absolutely convinced that he'd turn up there. She asked me to help her write letters to him, describing how she would furnish the van when it was chosen – the curtains, where the baby would sleep. Her plans on returning to Newbury were as optimistic and detailed as Davies returning to Sidcup in *The Caretaker*.

She had arrived in the home with absolutely nothing, and we all rustled round to kit her out with the odd jumper or skirt. Every day she took our orders for newspapers and went to the shops for little errands, cigarettes, sweets. Some of us gave her something for going, so she had a little pocket money.

Most people had applied for supplementary benefit for their stay in the home. A few had not. I was one of them. I didn't want to go into the welfare system. I would manage the £4.10s per week from my savings, and doggedly refused help – although Reverend Mother often gently suggested that perhaps pride was getting in the way of sense. She became used to me appearing in her office on Thursday with my envelope of cash.

Gradually as in any group, some of us were more drawn to each other and found comfort in conversation and discussion about our common predicament.

Jo, of course, was a great confidante. Also Jenny, a pottery teacher from Manchester, a very gentle, spiritual girl. Oona, a housekeeper from Dublin and Jeannette who worked in a bank and lived across the road from the convent. I'm not sure why she lived with us. Maybe it was a way of presenting the neighbours with a *fait accompli*, rather than putting up with months of whispers and speculation. Of the five of us two had already decided to keep their babies – Jeannette and Oona. Oona was planning to work as a residential housekeeper in a job that accepted a baby. Jeannette came from a big family, lots of brothers and her mother loved the idea of another baby.

Jeannette's mother often invited us to their house and listened to our anguished heart-searching, dried our tears and gave us tea.

Sometimes when I'd spent time with her I would think, Why don't I ring my mother now? Tell her what's happened to me, and she'll sort everything out. Then I would start to imagine what it would mean to them – the Catholic headmaster – the mistress of morals and discipline in a Catholic school.

I knew what she'd say, what she would do. She would be briefly devastated, then she'd make plans to accommodate you, to welcome you, house you, feed you, defend you from all harm, all criticism. She would be a lioness – no one would dare attack this new member of the family.

The sense of family loyalty has always been so powerful amongst the Callanans. Witness the rare ménage they had established for mutual support. Considering the volatile nature of the members of the commune, it seemed to work well, though not without its moments of strife. Dada gave a great deal to make it a success. He gave up independence, but in return he gained support and a little stake in a minute piece of England.

When you were about to be born, Claire was ten, dealing with the advantages and disadvantages of being the only child amongst five adults. On the plus side she always had someone to turn to for sympathy, if the parents were in a mood. She also had expert help from four teachers, with a broad spectrum of knowledge. She also had quintuple portions of birthday and Christmas presents.

On the minus she had the burden of five pairs of adult eyes constantly focused on her one small self; all those disciplinarians for one pupil. Not to mention her bossy older sisters! Auntie tells a story against herself of chastising Claire one day and she putting a paper carrier over her head and screaming: 'You're not the judge.'

I tried to imagine how you would make out in this ménage. Not so good, I feared, not so good.

I would have to find another solution. I now realized that I had for the first time considered, positively and realistically, the possibility of keeping you with me. Being with other girls in the same position, discussing how to look at all kinds of options, had opened my eyes and given me a kind of wild hope.

I asked Molly to buy *The Lady*, a fabled source of residential jobs and also on Sunday to get all the papers with competitions. 'Spot the Ball' in the *News of the World* would be the best. The £1000 prize would keep us going for a year without me working if Dada went on paying for the flat in London.

About this time too, Marie forwarded a letter from a director offering me two episodes of *Z Cars*. I calculated that I would earn twenty-six pounds for each of these. Fifty-two pounds could put us on the road to independence. They were to be rehearsed and recorded round the time you would be five weeks old.

I rushed to Sister Theresa and asked if I could arrange for you to be looked after in the nursery while I did the work, and then take you home. She must have been accustomed to this kind of madness amongst her girls, because she didn't dismiss the whole idea as ludicrous outright. But she gently suggested that two episodes of *Z Cars* was not a long-term solution and that apart from my emotional state after you were born, I might not physically be up to it.

I used to tell you each day what I'd done or planned and with what success. Sometimes I chatted to you in the room when Jo was off elsewhere but mostly I'd find a quiet spot in the garden, on a sunny day and speak undisturbed.

I still had no idea whether you were a boy or a girl and used to call you Gloria or Mavis or George as the mood took me!

Jo had more or less decided that it was best for her baby to be adopted. She came from a very close community and felt the scrutiny would be intolerable – added to which her father was in a state of shock.

Jenny saw no other course but adoption. Her family were very religious and pillars of the community. They felt that to have an illegitimate child in the family would be devastating, not only to Jenny but to her sisters. She was hoping her baby would be a boy because there were none in the family. To give a boy away, she felt, would be less traumatic than losing a girl. A boy would be a stranger. A girl would be family.

Looking back at the wild logic we all indulged in, it's a wonder we didn't all go off our heads. We were all dealing with emotions on so many levels. With shame first of all. But shame about what? About having committed the sin in the first place? Or the shame of having been found out? Guilt. Terrible guilt we all felt at having placed a child in this precarious position. Guilt for the anguished burden many of us had placed upon our families, their hopes for us dashed, their reputations ruined. Not for my family so far, they still had no idea how I was really spending my summer. And grief – still to come for us, grief. We saw it in the eyes of those who left before us, mostly in the late morning, waving goodbye, hugging, unable to really help them as they walked down the path to sorrow.

The value of that safe haven of the convent was incalculable. For the six weeks before and the six weeks after your birth, I would be cocooned from all harm and all judgement. I would be properly fed and medically cared for in a loving environment by those wonderful nuns. The only thing they couldn't protect me from was myself. In the end only I could take responsibility for our lives, yours and mine. They couldn't protect me from my dutiful, loyal, logical, illogical, demented, intransigent self.

One of the loveliest moments in the home was when a new baby was born. Each time Sister Theresa or Sister Frances would come to the nursery window which overlooked the sitting-room, and hold up high the new arrival. They looked like small Egyptian mummies all swaddled in white.

We'd all move over to see if the little one was anything like his mother or the spit of the father we'd never seen. It's a strange thing but girls do have the stamp of their father on them the moment they're born.

I remember when Heidi's baby arrived Sister Frances was worried about him. Although he was a robust and cheerful seven and a half pounds, he had a greyish colour and she kept listening to his heart, massaging his limbs, and checking his mouth for mucus congestion. She was on the point of whipping him off to hospital when she had a flash of inspiration.

'Heidi,' she said to the drowsy German girl, 'is it possible your baby's father was Indian?'

'No, Sister,' said Heidi as she drifted off. 'Definitely Pakistani. Karachi. That's in Pakistan.'

Sighs of relief all round.

I hadn't been tremendously aware of babies till this time. I'd been excited and thrilled when Claire was born, but not being a looker in prams, I thought they all came out more or less uniformly pink or brown, with closed eyes and no hair. Wrong.

First, they varied enormously in size from tiny brave James Joseph who went straight into the hospital at two and a half pounds, to an eleven-pound girl for little Dawn. And the hair! All kinds of hair: black electric shock spikes, red curls, long enough to put a bow in, sprouts like Tintin. They immediately developed personalities. We all knew every baby's cry and problems as well as our own. We knew the starving ones, the idle grizzlers, the ragers and the lonely ones.

The nursery was immaculate and very organized. Every mother had a feeding chair and a cot and shared the baths and sinks at the end of the room. It was cleaned on the rota and bottles were prepared in the milk kitchen. So it was a very peaceful entry into motherhood. Nappies and bedding were washed in the laundry. Babies were fed at six, ten, two, six and ten, and after the night feed everyone had a good seven hours' sleep while the night nurses took over.

Around my fourth week at the convent, Sister Theresa asked me if I'd organize an entertainment for Reverend Mother's Feast Day (more and more like a very nice convent boarding-school!). I had about ten days to prepare it. I think she had in mind a couple of songs, maybe a poem or two and something on the piano. But I wanted to offer something a bit more unusual to thank them for their incredible kindness.

I decided to arrange the show in two halves. Part One

would indeed be songs and poems and piano. But then there would be an interval for tea, after which we would present: 'The most Lamentable Comedy and most Cruel Death of Pyramus and Thisbe'. This play within a play from *A Midsummer Night's Dream* was a sure-fire crowd pleaser. My mother had often used it to introduce her pupils to Shakespeare, and I thought it would be easy to cobble some sets and costumes together. Carbon off the words, give out some parts and away we'd go. I reckoned without a marked reluctance on the part of any of my fellow inmates to perform. Most of the mothers pleaded lack of sleep, lack of time, lack of talent, and the antenatals said they were too embarrassed by their bumps.

However, I persisted and finally had the first half set with Heidi on the guitar, Elizabeth on the piano and Bernadette and me singing Irish songs. No poems, but never mind.

Eventually by bullying and cajoling I forced Jo into Pyramus, I would play Thisbe. Molly was desperate to play Wall but couldn't read the lines, let alone learn them. So she took on Moon – magnificently. Vicky, who was still at school, responded to the teacher in me and rehearsed into a great Wall.

My friend Rosanna did sterling sewing work with old sheets in between her kitchen job.

On the day, the community came into the sitting-room about 3 p.m., along with everybody who wasn't feeding a baby or having one – a quiet day for labour fortunately.

The first half went really well; lovely guitar from Heidi, Bernadette singing a rebel song; me, 'She Moved Through the Fair'. A surprise item from quiet Maura who played a haunting harmonica and for the finale Elizabeth dazzled us all by playing 'Clair de Lune' wonderfully with those slim, manicured fingers.

Everyone was delighted by the show so far but amazed to hear there was yet more after a break. Jo had organized a catering team to serve a little afternoon tea, while we set up for the play, and about twenty-five minutes later we launched into 'Pyramus and Thisbe'.

Now, over the past two weeks I had experienced every emotion known to a director. (The only time I've ever been one.) I'd known hope, despair, pity, disbelief, rage (so much so that Sister Theresa ventured to suggest I was pushing the reluctant thespians too hard) and finally resignation.

It's a well-tried fail-safe formula, the amateur drama group, but when the hour came all those girls gave a performance that was so committed, wholehearted, I would've cried if I hadn't been laughing so much.

It's extraordinary how a little response from an audience can work wonders with even the most timid performer. One good shriek from Sister Bernard and away they went. Forgotten the agonies of learning lines, of standing up in front of people; forgotten even the big stomachs and tomorrow's sorrows. They spoke and moved like a group of old pros. Molly's Moon face shone so much I thought she'd burst into flames.

'I'm going to tell him all about this when I get back to Newbury.'

Back to reality.

It was a great day though.

Jo went into labour a couple of days later. She swore it was the effort of the show. She had terrible back pain and a very long labour, but when I went up to see her after Grace was born, she had completely forgotten it. She was quite transfigured. I'd noticed it before in the other girls – a kind of softening, a moving into another reality – but Jo was someone I'd become really close to and loved – and now she was different.

'No one's taking her away from me. No one's going to take her away.'

Jo's eyes and Grace's were locked together by an invisible laser. Anyone who's had a child knows that look

– 'bonding' it's now called. Magic, I thought then.

I saw Jo was no longer wearing her elaborate eye make-up – she never did again – didn't need to. I felt alone.

Later on that day, Rosanna asked me to look after her baby, Francesca, for the two daytime feeds during the next few days. She was keeping Francesca and needed to go for job interviews as a residential housekeeper. Everybody breastfed their babies to give them the sweetest possible start in life, so Rosanna had to express milk for two feeds each day. She showed me what kind of shaped nappy Francesca wore, how to wind her, how to make her smile. She was a beautiful, dainty creature with dark curly hair and immaculately dressed in hand-embroidered frocks.

It was extraordinary being in the nursery, very peaceful, despite the ten or so babies; odd bits of conversation but mostly each mother firmly focused on her child.

Even Maureen, belligerent and wary, denying up to the last moment that she was pregnant, sat feeding her monstrous boy who was nicknamed Bulldog, with something like pride on her face.

I'm thirteen years older than my sister Claire so I knew a bit about babies and Francesca was charming and responsive to anything I did for her. I was sad when my time *in loco parentis* came to an end and I handed her back to Rosanna.

It was Friday 26 June and I knew you were due on the 28th. I suddenly became galvanized into action, only two days to get everything ready.

I took out all the clothes I'd prepared for you. Washed all the new nappies and the bath towels, handwashed all the clothes and aired and ironed them. By Friday evening everything was ready and I was knackered!

During the night Jeannette went into labour and fairly quickly had a terrific baby boy. One of those boys who look butch from the moment they're born. Her mother was delighted. Jeannette was due the same day as me, so I was a bit fed up when by Saturday night there wasn't a hint that you were ready to be born.

On Sunday there was a bit of a flurry early in the morning when Danielle started to have labour pains. She'd not long arrived and her baby wasn't due for a good six weeks or so.

Danielle was very thin and chirpy with a little, pretty, starveling face, which became even more pinched when she had a pain. Sister Frances examined her and decided that there was no immediate evidence of a baby being born and that it might even be a false alarm.

Sister Frances decided it would be all right for her to go to Mass and asked if I'd keep Danielle company. Sister Theresa was in church already, and one of the other girls who was a nurse had not yet come on duty.

It was pretty quiet on the labour floor, only Jo asleep, Jeannette, resting after the birth, and Oona up in her room, due the same day as me, and not feeling too good.

I sat with Danielle and told her how fed up I was that she'd beaten me to it; gave her a drink of lemon juice; tried to distract her from the pains! I talked about my family and hers. At first she found chatting easy between pains but then I noticed gradually a very strained look about her.

'I wanna go to the toilet.'

'OK, I'll get a bedpan, don't move.'

I hustled round and found one, pushed it under her and covered her up for privacy. After a bit the pain subsided, and she said she didn't want to go any more. I'd scarcely taken the bedpan out, when she shouted again: 'I wanna go to the toilet.'

This happened a couple more times with increasing urgency before I realized that she was trying to push the baby out.

'Don't push, Danielle, breathe quickly. Do you mind if I have a look to see what's happening?'

'No, go on.'

It's funny how we preserve these little niceties, even in times of crisis. Neither of us was embarrassed, so I took a quick peek.

To my horror I could see the baby's head about two inches in diameter.

'I wanna go to the toilet.'

'Don't push, Danielle. Breathe quickly.'

I rushed to the door and shouted for Oona who came staggering along the corridor.

'Quickly, get Sister Frances out of church. Tell her Danielle's baby's ready to be born.'

She moved like the wind, all fourteen stone of her.

Sister Frances rushed up, followed by Alice. By now Danielle was in real deep pain. I left her to the experts.

Pretty soon we learned that the baby was very premature, about ten weeks. A crisis unit arrived from the hospital and took both him and Danielle in.

Little James Joseph stayed there until a week before I left. I was glad to meet him. He was four pounds by then, lungs like a sergeant major and the biggest balls I've ever seen!

Winter 1962

Fame at last! Two episodes of Emergency Ward 10. *And now a* Twenty-Four Hour Call. *That was the important one because I got that on my own merits.*

The part of Nurse Elliot in Ward 10 *was written by Diana Morgan, mother of my friend, Derry Barbour, so that was a 'who you know' job. Wonderful though and a door opened that I'm sure would have remained forever closed to me. Thanks, Diana.*

I loved that job. I felt really green though. I had no idea about television, all the bittiness of it. I made a terrible gaffe in the first episode. Ward 10 *goes out live so you have to keep* on your toes. *Between my second and third scenes I was hanging around close so I wouldn't miss my entrance, and I was just walking into my next set or so I thought. I went through the door, all sets look alike from behind, and found myself surrounded by lights, cameras, and – a live scene. Oh God. It was between Jill Browne and a patient. I saw her looking a bit alarmed so I took a deep breath and marched over to the bed, took a thermometer out of its glass, shook it and walked out of the door, puce and shaking.*

'Thank you, nurse,' said Jill as I left her to get on with her scene.

I was dead from embarrassment when I apologized later, but she was lovely, very kind. Desmond Carrington too gave me a special hug when he found out it was my first television.

Mostly during rehearsals I palled up with the other girls, Ilona, Carol, Beverly. Beverly has been acting for ever, knows everybody. One day as we walked into the studios, we bumped into Julia Foster, looking glam and casual in a huge soft fluffy jumper.

'H'ya Bev. How's things?'

'All right. This is a nice one I'm doing. How about you?'

'I've got a series, lucky, eh?'

'You lucky bugger, deserve it too. See ya.'

I wish I knew more people. I wish I could say a quick hello to Julia Foster without looking stagestruck. It's all so incredibly new and glamorous, I find it hard to stop my jaw hanging open.

The canteen at ATV is huge; a bar and cafeteria and lots of noise and famous people, and all the while the tannoy blares out. I sat there with Bev on taping-day of my second episode.

'Patrick Wymark, telephone please.'

'Tommy Cooper, reception please.'

'John Alderton, telephone please.'

I watched a tall gangling young man with black hair slope past us.

'Who's he?' I asked Bev.

206

'Haven't you seen him? He's in our episode.'

'Oh yeah.'

'One of the new doctors. He hasn't got much this week. He's not in a lot.'

'Oh yes.' I remembered seeing him draped over one of the hospital beds in rehearsal. *'He looks nice – funny. I haven't talked to him. I must say hello.'*

I never got round to it though.

There's a lovely cameraman on this Twenty-Four Hour Call. *Ron Francis. I'm going to a party with him tonight. Great.*

Late on Monday night, Oona had a girl, very beautiful, creamy skin, black hair, long legs and long eyelashes, just like her mother. One by one the new girls had become old girls, wiser girls. It was curious to see different emotions coming into play as the girls became mothers. The Oona I first knew was, although in her twenties, like a big kid, a hockey captain of a girl, rumbustious, funny – immediate. Overnight she matured five years. She was still witty and lovely, but she achieved a super efficiency, an assurance that left me dazzled. She even moved differently.

I woke on Tuesday 30th in my familiar room that I now shared with Jill, a sixteen year old who was getting married after her baby was born. The moment I awoke it was with a feeling of indescribable novelty. I felt as though I was about to jump off a cliff into space. It was elation and terror all intermingled.

'I think I'm in labour,' I said to Jill. She was less than fascinated by this news. It was ten to five in the morning, and she didn't want to know.

'Ah, good,' turned over and went back to sleep.

I couldn't sleep so I got up, had a bath very quietly and padded downstairs. Alice, getting ready to come off night duty, was making a cup of tea in the milk kitchen.

'Give us a cup, Alice.'

'Sure, no sugar?'

'No, thanks. I think I'm in labour.'

'Grand. Have your waters broken?'

'No.'

'How often are the pains?'

'I haven't got any. Just a feeling.'

'Oh, sweetheart, wishful thinking.'

'I'm sure it's not that.'

'Let's have a feel.'

She laid her practised hand on the base of my stomach, felt and prodded gently, and shook her head.

'I don't think so. Maybe Sister can give you an internal later.'

'OK.'

After we'd had our tea I went round giving the mothers their wake-up calls for the six-o'clock feed, to give Alice a break. She still had five weeks to go herself and had volunteered to do night duty for Bernadette who was getting married the next week in the convent chapel.

Everyone was madly excited. Bernadette was a great favourite with the nuns. She was a wonderful and tireless nurse and they were delighted that she and Patrick had finally decided to get married and make a home for Anthony who was now three months old and had spent some time in the nursery while she worked. It was to be a white wedding; she had a lovely dress with a train made by one of the nuns. And the community had organized a reception for her in the convent dining-room.

When the last straggler had tottered down in her quilted dressing-gown, I was at a loose end and went up to the labour ward to see if anyone was awake and interested in my unfounded presentiments.

I looked in on Jo and found her fast asleep, tucked up with Grace. The arrangements were more loose in that first week. If the mother felt up to it she could keep her baby close by her. If she was fatigued or groggy, the labour ward nursery was just around the corner. Maura was on duty on the labour floor, sitting in a chair with Oona's Siobhan. Oh how much longer till I could be here too?

After I'd had breakfast and done my jobs, I thought I'd have another opinion on the state of play and got Sister Theresa to examine me. She agreed that you were definitely ready to be born, head firmly in place, and all systems go, but there were as yet no sure-fire signals, no dilation, no pains, no broken waters.

'Let's just see how we go, I'll look at you again, later.'

There's nothing more all-consuming than waiting for a baby to come, impossible to concentrate on anything except the imminent new person. I wanted to talk to you alone, and was glad that Jill had gone to town after lunch. We would have the bedroom to ourselves. It was a very hot June day and all the windows were open. There was a wonderful smell in the air, blossom with little drifts of the lunch-time cooking still lingering, and the birds very loud.

I read recently in an otherwise very good piece of esoteric writing that the soul doesn't enter the body until the baby is born. I can't believe that's true.

The youness of you had been my constant companion for at least three months. I knew you. It was interesting to know whether you were a boy or a girl, but it made no difference to your essence. I knew you. I already knew that you were curious and responsive. That when I sang you liked it. Danced even. I knew that you were sometimes lonely in the middle of the night and gave me a nudge so that I would tuck my arm back under my stomach around you.

I knew too that you were old for your age, burdened by my hopeless tears on the black days. Then you would be very quiet and still. Neither kick nor bounce. Oh, you were good.

You were very quiet too on this June day, as I began to talk.

'Well, Gloria–George, it's no use lying doggo. This is the day.'

No answer.

'I haven't won Spot the Ball.'

Oh really.

'I love you. I don't know what to do. But I love you. Please be born.'

Still, still.

I went to the wardrobe and got your wicker case out and smoothed out all your clothes on the bed. I put all the nighties and dresses on hangers and hung them from the curtain rail in the sunshine. I put a towel on the window sill and laid the vests and jackets in a row.

Then I lay on my bed and closed my eyes for a moment, listening to the afternoon. The radio in the sitting-room drifted upwards through the summer windows. Top of the hit parade.

'You're my world. You are my night and day. You're my world, you're every breath I take.' Cilla Black.

Suddenly you gave me the most almighty shove, pressed me on some nerve or other that sent a shooting pain right through me. I sat up. Stood up. Bent down. Didn't know what to do. Then it stopped.

Then – a little rhythmic nag. So you were listening. Thanks, chuck.

I was in labour. Only just. A little show. Very low key, very infrequent pains, but we were on our way. Sister Theresa told me to time the pains if they got more frequent or intense but they didn't.

Tea-time turned to supper and I wandered round the garden with Jenny who was hugely pregnant and already a week overdue.

'I'm sure it's a girl,' said Jenny. 'You look nice,' she said. 'Quite smart.'

I was wearing my 'best' pregnancy outfit, the red dress and bedroom slippers!

'I feel a bit rough, but I'm excited. Would you like this

dress after I've finished with it? I haven't worn it much.'

'I'd love it. I'm sick to death of my stuff.'

We went in for our late-night drink and I went up to the labour ward for an examination. Bernadette looked me over.

'Hardly dilated at all. When was the last pain?'

'About an hour and a half ago.'

'I think you're all right till morning. I'll give you something to help you sleep.'

I never took sleeping pills and this one put me out like a light.

'Good night, Bernadette.'

'Night and God bless.'

I was awoken out of a deep torpor by a terrific pain and a gush of warm water from between my legs. I got out of bed. Very difficult. It was a high hospital bed and I was shell-shocked from the pill, I could hardly stand, didn't know what day it was. I staggered out of the room towards the nursery.

'Maura, I think my water's broken.'

'God, let's have a look.'

Back to the bed, Maura examining me.

'God you're crowning. Hold on, I'll get Sister Frances.'

A blur. I felt as though I was seeing myself from outside.

Sister Frances arriving hastily dressed and she and Maura heaved me on to the labour table. Bits of conversation.

'The waters must have broken about twelve-fifteen.'

Terrific burning like very bad period pain.

'You'll be ready to push soon, Pauline, just try to breathe deeply when there's a pain.'

Sister Frances's calm soft voice.

'All right, now on the next pain, give a good push.'

I do.

211

'There's a good girl.'

I fall asleep for a while. Seconds.

'Now another lovely push. There now.'

Maura and Sister Frances holding my legs and stroking and patting in between. Calm. This goes on for some time. An eternity. I'm pushing till I'm red in the face but the pain is no less severe and I feel no progress.

Sister listening to your heartbeat, monitoring my futile efforts. A bit worried. After the next big failure I hear words.

'Rigid perineum.'

'Episiotomy.'

I hear metal. I am mostly asleep but see a kidney dish and scissors.

'A little snip, Pauline,' says Sister Frances. 'To help the baby out.'

I don't feel it but on the next push suddenly a glorious sensation.

You are born! At least your head.

'Don't push, don't push.'

Panic words, 'Foetal distress.'

'The cord. The cord is round the neck.'

Here comes another contraction.

'Pant, don't push. I have it, I have it. All right, push.'

I push and there you are, shot on to my leg like a baby dolphin. Quarter to two.

'It's a little girl.'

I am suddenly completely focused. The drug can no longer touch me, I am awake, alert. I see you. I reach down to your head, stroke the damp, catch your hand. You are perfect. You are very neat and sweet and beige beneath the blood. I want to hold you but then you are overtaken by Maura helping you to breathe, clearing your mouth, cutting the cord. Taking you away to wash you. The afterbirth is delivered and Sister Frances tells me in the morning the doctor will come to stitch me. Maura brings you to me in a labour-ward frock and shawl. I hold you in the crook of my left arm and cannot move my eyes from you. You are beautiful.

'Hello.'

I put my finger in your hand. You hold it very tightly and then open your eyes and stare at me. You know me. I told you I knew you. It is the magic. Then we fall asleep, you and I. A little later Maura takes you away.

'We have to keep an eye on her for a bit,' she whispered. 'I'll bring you a cup of tea.'

I want to talk to you but you're in another room. Maybe I'll wander along to the nursery and watch over you. I sit up bright with intention, then the brain gives in, succumbs to the sleeping pill. I am blank.

In the morning Reverend Mother came in to visit.

'I've just seen Gloria. She's a very pretty baby.'

I looked at her and laughed.

'She's not Gloria, she's Louise.'

'Molly told me it was Gloria, lovely name.'

'It was just a nickname – Gloria–George.'

Reverend Mother mystified. I'm not laughing any more. Maybe her mother's called Gloria – or George!

'But she's really Louise.'

'That's nice too.' Sister Frances comes in.

'There now, how are you?'

'Fine, still a bit sleepy.'

'What's the matter with her eye, Sister Frances?'

'Whose eye?' I'm alarmed.

'Ah, she tried to push the baby out through her eyes.' Sister Frances showed me a mirror. I looked like Frankenstein's auntie, one eye was completely blood-filled. I'd broken a capillary with all that fruitless pushing.

'Where's the baby?'

'We'll bring her in now. Just try putting her to the breast, but she's still a very tired little soul.'

Then there you were, still in the labour-ward trousseau, dozing in the arms of Sister Theresa. Sister placed your head firmly at the breast and placed the nipple in your mouth. It was still strange to me to be physically cared for by a nun. All my long experience of the religious orders was of a very spiritual nature. Nuns were super-human, living on a plane so rarefied I would have been astonished at Hammersmith to have ever seen them eat. They moved with a glide that was almost ghostlike. Yet here was Sister Theresa teaching you, teaching me, something that would be denied to her. Such love, such generosity.

She tickled your toes – patted your cheek. Then whoosh – a white light rocked my being as you started to suckle. Then the eye lock.

'Good girl,' said Sister Theresa.

To you? Or me? We worked together perfectly. Just a little feed on each side and then you dropped into a heap. We slept together till the doctor came and they took you away while he stitched me.

Nice man. Humiliating experience. Up went my legs in stirrups while he did his drawn threadwork and chatted companionably about politics, the Beatles. I felt like a terrible gross turkey, powerless in a roasting tin, embarrassed, speechless. Please let this end. It did.

All the girls who'd gone before us warned me to make the most of that week on the labour floor. Never again would we have such peace, such undiluted time with our babies. It was the beginning of a uniquely happy six weeks. In the midst of the most traumatic experience of our lives we managed, you and I, to cocoon a portion of ourselves and make a little lifetime of suspended reality in which we were happy. I wasn't alone in this. Sister Frances and Sister Theresa treated us all the same, regardless of our future plans.

Sorrow and despair were acknowledged but shown into another room. Our whole focus was on giving each of our children everything we could possibly offer in that six weeks.

It was the norm for every baby to be breastfed whether or not she was to stay with her mother, and to remain together for six weeks. In the beginning, some girls thought this was very tough but with one exception, none of us regretted it. Each baby was loved and cared for by her own mother until the day she was handed to her new parents. The blessing of this was that the babies were properly bonded with their own mothers. The sorrow was that the separation was all the more devastating to mother and child.

But that was yet to come, pushed away, disregarded in our safe haven.

The week on the labour floor was wonderful. There were four of us, friends together, Jeannette, Jo, Oona and I. We were joined by Jenny who was beginning to despair, under observation.

I wrote to Tony in St Andrews to tell him you were born – that you were called Louise, that you looked very like him.

I was still shutting him out from any decisions about your future. I must have been incredibly arrogant, stubborn. I used him shamelessly to compound my story to the family that I was on an extended tour. Got him to post my letters in Scotland. Yet I wouldn't let him into our lives.

By Sunday I was full of wild plans and sent Molly for every paper with competitions, and the usual copy of *The Lady*. I entered every competition in every paper that week and for the next five Sundays. I promised Molly a cut when I won. Every week we'd check the winners together and every week Molly would raise her doleful eyes in question: 'No luck?'

'No luck, Mol.'

The extra load must have been too much for Molly. She went into labour that night and had a thin little boy very like her.

We had established an easy routine, you and I, not

remarkable in essence, wash, eat, sleep, wash, eat, sleep, several times a day, but special in small ways. I thought your progress in that first week was remarkable but then so do all mothers.

It was wonderful to see you in the bath. After an initial shriek of affront when the water lapped around your body, you got very excited, and loosed and flexed starfish hands, breathing quickly.

You loved songs too, even stopped eating to listen. 'Summertime', George Gershwin – rapt attention. 'Skye Boat Song'. Certain phrases made your lip quiver, the notes of chord change touching somewhere very deep.

I had some awful dreams that week though, one vivid and recurring.

Mama was trussed up on a labour table like a chicken, legs folded back over her shoulders. She was alive but only just. You were in a white lacy cradle on wheels, that kept sliding out of the room, down a long tunnel towards the ferry boats and the river.

Part of my old childhood dream. I was trying to untie Mama and running to and fro trying to catch the cradle. One night the cradle rolled on to the ferry boat. But the Captain wouldn't let me on because I hadn't paid, and you sailed without me.

Dreams apart, the peace of the first week of the little upstairs world was sorely missed when I came down on Thursday, back to work, not arduous but time-consuming, and a different routine. We were less together in the mornings, you in the nursery, me washing the corridor floor outside, and I could hear you crying, much more hungry these days and obviously not satisfied with what I had to offer. It wasn't too bad in the afternoons. All the babies went out in prams in the garden and you could easily have a little extra snack in the shade of a tree. But at six and again at ten you were squealing with hunger.

Sister Theresa test-weighed you a few times and suggested that I try to persist in the hope that my milk would be more plentiful or at least of a better quality. I drank pints of milk, took vitamins and worried. All to no avail. Halfway through your third week, you began to have a little top up in a bottle.

I could hardly wait to see you each morning. Jo and I were together again, but in a little room next to the Visitors' Room which is an annexe across from the main building. We were called around five-thirty by whoever was on duty. Sometimes they gave us a tea. I liked being there because I could take you in the afternoon and lie on the bed with you on my chest, endlessly searching for a solution. You were very alert, brighter by the day. Your head was already quite erect. One of the nurses called you Noddy because you were always looking around, lovely round head nodding as you moved.

We'd all move around in an unstrained silence in those summer dawns, gradually coming to as all the babies settled into peaceful suckling, marvelling at the variety of little people we'd produced.

We were all a bit worried about Molly's baby, Raymond. He was still very puny and not very responsive, with a woebegone expression like an old man. His progress was not helped by the way Molly fed him. She tucked him virtually upside down under one arm and allowed the milk to more or less drop into him. She took the job very seriously and continued this way despite lots of advice from us all, until we became hysterical with laughter. We had visions of the milk eventually pouring out of poor Raymond's ears because certainly very little of it was reaching his stomach! In the end Sister Theresa sorted her out and fixed Raymond up with some extra nosh from a bottle. Pretty soon he was quite a round old thing.

By the time you were three and a half weeks old I'd applied for five jobs in *The Lady*. Three of them didn't reply, one of them sounded promising. It was as a housekeeper–companion to a lady in her fifties, 'Child

Accepted!' I rang the number and spoke to a very doubtful woman, explaining my situation. She agreed yes, that she would accept a child, but that she only liked girls. I said, well this was lucky because that's what you were. She further qualified her opinion that she didn't like noisy children, only quiet, well-behaved ones. I said in all honesty I couldn't vouch for your standard of behaviour at this early stage and gave her up as a bad job.

The second person who replied to me sounded really nice. 'Camilla' sent a very friendly letter describing the family and the job. She had three children, two, seven and nine, and they lived in Shropshire where she and her husband ran a building business together. She was pleased I was a trained teacher because she needed someone who could take an interest in the children's schoolwork and help them scholastically as well as having full-time charge of them. It wasn't exactly a cushy number, but her friendliness was appealing.

I rang her that evening. She was very pleasant, very county, asked if I could come for an interview and bring 'the scrap' with me. She said that she'd made some enquiries and there was a 'super' nursery for you quite near the children's school, and you could actually stay on a nightly basis if things got a bit hectic. She would help with the fees.

'I'm a bit confused,' I said. 'Does your baby go to the nursery?'

'No, we like them to be at home till they're four.'

'Well, I was rather hoping that Louise could be with me while I did this job.'

'I know,' said Camilla. 'But I feel there might be a conflict of interest if you've actually got two little ones to look after during the day and your "little scrap" would be jolly well cared for there.'

I made some polite noises, gave Camilla my regrets, and put the phone down.

How could anybody be so insensitive? I understood

her point of view, but why even contemplate someone with a child in the first place? And I absolutely hated her calling you 'the scrap' – it conjured a Dickensian image of a foundling child, waiting for the bits from the rich man's table.

I sat on the floor by the phone and cried. This wasn't going to work. The mental picture I had of some benevolent employer giving us a salary and a small but charming self-contained flat in exchange for an honest day's work was not going to happen. At best you would be tolerated by some hard-pressed working mother, desperate for a Mother's Help.

This was not for you. I didn't want you to grow up in someone else's house, an object of pity, of conjecture, a recipient of patronizing bounty and hand-me-down clothes. I think I was a snob.

I went in for your ten-o'clock feed with swollen eyes. Nobody mentioned it, no one asked why. It was a sight all too commonplace. We gave each other all that was needed, we girls, little things; a bottle fetched, a wet napkin taken away to the bucket; just something that said, 'We're here if you need us.'

You were awake but not crying when I went in, almost a smile when you saw me. Excited legs.

'Hallo, old thing.' I scooped you up into my arms and watched you eat – frowning a bit at me. I always found you remarkably tuned in to my highs and lows. We were still in fairyland, still shutting out the real world but it was becoming harder to ignore reality.

The next day Jo made me go into town with her, something, anything, for a change of perspective. I hadn't been outside the grounds since I'd arrived. We got two of the antenatals to keep an eye on our sleeping daughters after the two-o'clock feed.

I felt quite disorientated at first. I hadn't been on a bus, in a shop, amongst people, for weeks. Everything seemed very loud; traffic, voices, men. I hadn't seen men for ages, apart from the chaplain, the doctor and the tramps. Children in particular looked very odd, especially babies of about eighteen months. They seemed huge, grotesque even, after our neat little newborns.

I suppose I felt a bit like a prisoner must feel when he's let out, filled with a mixture of wonder and terror. We had a lovely couple of hours. In C & A I bought a little pink jacket for you and a white cotton dress for myself. It was wonderful to be thin again. I looked quite nice.

About four o'clock we plonked ourselves in a tea shop and had a real afternoon tea, scones and cream and all.

That evening after supper, Jo and I and Oona and Maura got dressed up: me in my new white dress, and went to a very respectable hotel-pub just round the corner from the convent.

We had a couple of very innocuous cocktails, some peanuts and crisps, and felt like a million dollars. Our lives had been so circumscribed, so single-focused, we'd forgotten what it was like to be chatted up, and almost without noticing found ourselves the target of three extremely average-looking blokes. Starved as we were of male company we quite enjoyed the attention, and after another round their predictable jokes began to seem riotously funny. We were all getting along fine when Oona suddenly said: 'Come on girls, ten to ten.'

We all fell off our bar stools and made our way to the door.

'You're not going?'

'We ain't even started yet.'

We assured them we absolutely had to leave, but they wouldn't let us go, barring the way with terylene armpits. We dodged under and round and set off towards home. But still they followed us.

'What about a coffee then?'

'What about a snog?'

As we reached the convent gates, we stopped.

'Got to go now.'

'You ain' in there?' faces gobsmacked with disbelief. 'You don't live there.'

We'd told them we were air hostesses!

'Bloody hell! Bloody goody goodies! Little nuns.'

We slammed the gates behind us, shrieking with laughter. If only they knew!

One day when you were just over four weeks old I was sitting under the tree at the far end of the garden playing with you. You were lying on a blanket under the great green umbrella, arms and legs motoring with excitement. You loved the leaves and kept making little stabs in their direction, staring at them, every now and then dodging the bits of sun that shot through the dapple.

Sister Theresa came round the back of the house with a family, mother, father, girl and boy aged around seven and nine. A handsome family, laughing, talking animatedly to Sister and to each other. Both the children had bright red hair. Sister Theresa waved and they started to walk towards us. They all came and joined me on the grass and the children played with you, tickling your toes and making you smile.

'This is how big I was when you got me, isn't it, Mum?' Amy smiled at her mother.

'No, you were much bigger. You were a roly-poly butterball.'

'I wasn't.' Sam threw himself across his mother's lap. 'I was weeny, because I was sick. And my real mum was. She was sick. That's why she asked you to be my mum, didn't she, Mum?'

'Yes, and weren't we lucky, Dad and I.'

'Yeah,' Sam pushed his dad over into a heap. 'You got me.'

'And you come every year, don't you?' said Sister Theresa.

Tranquil Amy stroked your furry head. 'We want to remember where we were born.'

Mrs McNamara turned to me: 'We've never made a

big secret of them being adopted. Always explained how they came to be ours. I think it's important.'

I was dazzled by the openness of this family. Their obvious love for each other, all four, the respect for the children's original mothers was beautiful without being cloying.

Later on in the afternoon Sister Theresa and I talked about them. It was remarkable how like brother and sister the two looked with their flaming hair. It hadn't been planned. Sam had been an unborn hairy monkey when he was chosen to join them.

'Are families chosen much in advance then?' I really knew nothing about the process.

'Sometimes. It's often a bit hard for a child like Molly's who may have learning difficulties when he grows up. But actually he's been fixed up. Ah, they're a grand couple. Simple people a bit older than most, very patient, and they've no illusions about what they're getting. They'll just love Raymond for himself.'

Sister Theresa paused a bit and rubbed the back of her hand, turning her Bride of Christ ring round and round.

'No problem with a baby like Louise though.'

A little moment.

'There's a family waiting for her.'

Oh God.

'Professional people. They live in London. I believe the husband's a mathematician.'

'I'm no good at maths, I hate it.'

Suddenly I'm beaten, clutching at straws.

'Do the McNamaras want another baby? I wish she could have someone like them.' I am weeping and hopeless.

Sister Theresa is a rock for me.

'That's exactly what they are. Just that kind of people.'

Looking back I think it was that day, that moment, I finally took my head out of the sand and faced myself. I'd been ignoring reality, putting aside the fact that I had to make a decision, still hoping an angel would ride in on a cloud, and give me a box of miracles.

But none had come. No magic win in Spot the Ball; no perfect job within the pages of *The Lady*; no courage from within myself to face the family and ask for help.

I was beaten, inadequate, spiritless, hopeless. I had nothing to give you. I would give you away.

Jo left a couple of days later with her mother and father; Mum delighted and adoring her new grand-daughter, Dad subdued and uncommunicative. I think Jo had a tough road ahead but she had her mother's support, she would make it. She had a remarkable inner strength. I would miss her so much.

We'd had a final evening at Jeannette's, the old gang, in the middle of her huge and welcoming family. Mrs Lee made great bowls of curry. But for once not even Jeannette's handsome kindly brothers could lift me from the Slough of Despond. My shell joined in, but most of me was back with you in the nursery.

I could hardly bear to let you from my sight. I began to hate the morning work because it kept me from you. After the two-o'clock feed, I would gather you up and take you to my little room in the annexe and let you fall asleep on my chest. Jill was with me again but often out planning for her wedding. So I had the place to myself in the day.

I am becoming a little crazy in my grief. I talk to you incessantly whether you are awake or not. I cry. I beg your forgiveness for the outrage I am about to commit on both of us. Then I chastise myself for upsetting you and stem the flow.

I sing songs, lullabies to give you peace and a good memory to take with you.

And in those last few days I promise you that not a day will go by of my life that I do not speak your name and send a little bolt of love to you.

And it never has. Every day an arrow.

I also held on to the belief, desperate, wild and fanciful that I would see you again. Maybe not till I was very old. But one day. That one day when you wanted it, I'd be there.

The evening before we left the convent, I was in the Visitors' Room in the annexe, finishing packing your things. I had put you in borrowed bits for the night so everything would be ready and clean for tomorrow.

Rosanna had been helping me, ironing some of your clothes.

She admired your lawn dresses and the matinée jackets. She loved them.

'I 'spec she goin' to have lot of clothes now.'

'Probably.' I nodded distracted.

'New family. Plenty money, she have lotta clothes.'

'Yes.' I knew she wanted some of your stuff.

'Yellow pram suit's lovely. Too hot now. Too big.'

'Well, it'll fit her in the autumn.'

I didn't want to give away anything of yours. They were for you, chosen for you. All your little possessions. I felt mean. Maybe I would give her the pink C & A jacket. You were not a pink girl. Maybe.

Rosanna had not long gone when Sister Frances came in and sat with me. I could hardly bear to look at her. She had sustained me through periods of such emotion, I knew if I met her eyes I would be uncontrollable. I busied myself with folding nappies and croaked monosyllables at her.

As I told you before, the nuns offered unstinting support but never told us what decisions we should make about our babies. They never said, 'That is right – that is wrong.' Only we could do that.

But that night in her secret heart I think Sister Frances felt I might be making a wrong one. She came the nearest I've ever heard to opinion.

'Have your parents any other grandchildren?'

'No.'

'Maybe they should at least know about her?' She's tentative.

'I can't, Sister. I can't.' I look at her and weep.

'All right.' Gentle. She feels in her pocket, holds my hand and gives me a holy picture with a little affirmation on it: 'In much patience shall thy peace be.'

'Her family will love her so much. She'll be a much-loved child.'

I can no longer speak so Sister Frances puts her arm round me.

When I went to your cot on that morning, 16 August, you were already awake and smiled as I came near. It broke my heart.

I bathed you in the clear morning and you gasped and chuckled. I put you in another 'home' nightie for the time being. We didn't leave till eight-thirtyish so you'd go back to sleep for a while and be fully dressed just before the taxi came.

The air was heavy, quiet, as it always was when someone took the adoption road.

I sat down in my chair and gave you the last breastfeed. Although I was now taking drying-up tablets, I still had milk. It belonged to you.

After I'd put you back to sleep, I bathed and dressed and gathered our belongings. My two big cases had gone the day before. There was just a holdall and a carrier full of nappies and your wicker case.

I had some tea and toast, more out of habit than desire, and went to dress you. You were sleepy and reluctant. Too early, not ten o'clock. I gave you a little milk in a bottle and put your jacket on. Sister Theresa had given me a Miraculous medal and I had one for you. I wore mine and pinned yours to your jacket. We were ready to go.

Everyone gathered to wave me, Oona roaring-crying, hugged me. Jenny quiet, knowing she was next. Jeannette and her mum; and Molly, standing in a heap by the front door with a morning paper for me.

'Never did win Spot the Ball.'

'No, Molly.'

'Will yous come and see me in Newbury when we get the caravan?'

'I will, Molly.'

A kiss goodbye from the Sisters and we are gone.

I cannot say what the journey to Waterloo was like. I saw only you, sleeping all the way, mostly flat out like an old drunk, snoring a little; sometimes curling in a bit, truffling for milk in your dreams.

I was aware of some debs getting on at Reading, exclaiming over your minuteness and cuteness.

'Oooh, sweet.'

'Absolutely teeny!'

I may have responded, maybe not.

Clapham Junction. A sudden shock. I was within minutes of home. I could get off and run with you along the drive.

If the express stopped at Queens Road it would be a sign. It would be a sign that it was right for you to stay with me, right for you, not wrong for you to be my child.

The train was slowing down. I saw everything familiar. The Poly. Checkleys. The shops, the long sweep of the drive and the astonishing lushness of the midsummer park. The train was slowing down. If it stopped it would mean I should get off and we would walk along the drive, you and I, and let ourselves into the flat, and it would be right for you, not wrong for you, that all my familiars would be yours.

It must be incomprehensible to you now that I was waiting for some eleventh-hour miracle and never considered making my own.

The train was slowing down. I started to gather my things. Mad. It would stop. I saw the platform. I saw the sign. QUEENS ROAD, BATTERSEA. My hand was on the door.

An elderly man across from me moved forward a little urgently, detained my hand with his.

'Not here, love. Doesn't stop here.'

The sign gone, I sat down.

So be it.

We got out at Waterloo and took a taxi as the nuns had advised, a wild extravagance for such a short journey, but I was glad. London seemed jangling and dangerous after the convent.

The entrance to the Children's Society was an ecclesiastical-looking door on the back side of the Cathedral. I rang the bell and was let in by a nice girl with a sympathetic face and long dark hair. She showed me into a bleak room, furnished with a few straight chairs and a very soiled pram with no mattress or covers.

'Hello, I'm Hannah. Would you like to give baby her feed now and change her? I'll warm the bottle for you.'

'Yes, thank you.'

While she was gone, I started to make some kind of speech to you. We'd had many talks, you and I, over the weeks, desperately circling the situation, looking for the right thing to do. Now I only wanted to say 'I love you' over and over again. No point in explaining, excusing. I knew you well enough by now to know that at some very deep level you knew exactly what was happening.

A man came into the room and introduced himself as Mr Bagnell, the senior officer. He was a kindly man in a neat suit. Neat suits, it seemed were the order of the day. I had dressed carefully that morning, in one of navy-blue serge and a round-brimmed, navy straw hat. I wanted to look respectable. I wanted those in the Children's Society to impress upon your adoptive family that you were the daughter of someone respectable. I wanted them to think this child is special, precious, one in a zillion, not the offspring of a careless slag.

Wasn't I foolish? Your uniqueness needed no back up from me to tell them that.

My heart and head were pounding at such a rate that I only gradually began to realize that he was telling me about your new family. He said that they had already arrived and were waiting in another part of the building. He said your brother, who was four, was beside himself with excitement at the prospect of having a baby sister.

This was the first time I heard that you were to be part of a family who already had a child. In the midst of the agony, I felt a huge sense of relief. At least one of my major anxieties was allayed. I already knew that your prospective father was a mathematician, and my brain had churned over the possibility that they might be disappointed in you because, like me, you were poor at maths. When I look back, the ludicrous machinations of my mind were probably a desperate attempt to block the adoption course by all the means at my disposal.

Anway you were not, thank God, to be the sole recipient of all their hopes and ambitions.

As he talked about the family, I began to get a strangely vivid picture of the woman who was to become your mother. I had an image of someone as removed from me as she could be; fair where I was dark, slim where I was round, elegant where I was not. I also suddenly knew that however desolate the rest of my life would be, you would be all right, you would be – loved.

Hannah came in with the bottle and then the people left us alone for your last feed.

I took your bonnet off and stroked your very bald head, where the cradlecap had been. You sucked quite slowly on the bottle, frowning, still puzzled by this unfamiliar nipple. I held you closely and, bitterly regretting the unyielding serge suit, put your soft shawl between you and it.

When you'd had enough I sat you up and winded you as you nodded and bobbed in your sweet familiar fashion. Food usually made you drowsy-drunk, unable to keep your eyes open. But not today. You were still and wide awake and watchful and worried, as I laid you on two napkins from my bagful to protect you from the awful pram. I put your pull-ups on again, leaving off the ribbons which kept them up at the ankles, because they seemed tight.

I went back to sit on the chair and stumbled a bit, banging your head on the back of it. You cried, a very little, and I wanted to die from the awfulness of it. I said sorry and kissed you a hundred times. Then Mr Bagnell came back in.

He asked about your clothes and I gave them to him in the wicker picnic basket. There they were; two vests, two frocks, two jackets, three nighties and the other woollen suit, yellow like a baby chicken. The napkins were in another bag.

I also had one small tin of baby milk. For some reason, it had been suggested two days before I left that your new family would find this more convenient than the National Dried and I had bought some tins of milk. On the morning I left, only one remained.

'Well, that seems to be everything,' said Mr Bagnell.

I held you still in my arms.

'Will you tell her mother . . .' I had said it. I had acknowledged the truth. 'Will you tell her mother that she has a little birthmark on her right leg and that she mustn't worry, it will fade.'

'Yes, of course.' The man picked up the wicker case. 'Would you like to give me baby now?'

I stood up from the chair with you still enfolded in my arms. I must have been holding you quite tightly, but my arms felt disembodied from the rest of me, as if they were now part of you, and could no longer be detached from you.

The man put the basket down. 'Shall I take baby now?'

I stood while he took you and left the arms with me. He moved a little towards the other end of the room. I put a hand out.

229

'Don't go. Can I kiss her?' I was weeping, streaming.

He held you forward a little, and I kissed you, too discreetly with typical restraint, leaving some tears on your face. As I stepped back a little, he secured you on his left arm and picked up the basket in his right, backing towards a door I had not noticed before.

'Try not to upset yourself. Say goodbye to baby now.'

I made the awful sound and your arms jerked and you turned sharply to look at me – knowing, knowing, knowing. Then quickly through the door and that was the last time I saw you.

When you had gone I found myself quite unable to stop sobbing, quite rare for me, always in control.

Almost as soon as that door closed upon you, Hannah entered through the other and circled me sympathetically.

'Rough, isn't it?'

The understatement of the century. There is in me a kind of inbuilt politeness, a compulsion to respond to any form of communication. Even then. Even *in extremis*.

'Mmmh.' Awful, bubbling affirmative.

'Are you all right?'

All right? All wrong. All, all wrong. Not ever right again.

'Mmmh.'

'Would you like a cup of tea?'

'Mmmh. No, thank you.'

'Before you go.'

Where?

Mr Bagnell came back in again, taking the bag of nappies, and telling me how thrilled with you they are.

'Try to compose yourself. Is she going to have some tea?' he asked Hannah.

'No, thank you. I'm going.'

I moved about the room, gathering my goods; hand-bag, also navy blue, and my little holdall, that had held your bottles. I started to fold the wet napkin I'd left in the pram.

'No, that's all right, leave that,' said Hannah.

'I think you'd better have some tea,' said he. 'It'll give you time to compose yourself.'

A few minutes later when I was escorted to the Ladies to wash my face, I realized it would also give them time to show you and your new family off the premises without the danger of us meeting.

Again the powerful image of the slim fair woman – elegant and loving. I wanted to rush out and see her. Not to frighten her but to say thank you for the huge generosity of spirit that moved in her. I didn't even try. Such a contact was absolutely forbidden.

Half an hour after I'd handed you over for ever, I walked out into the traffic – literally. Into the path of a lorry, oblivious to the screeches of the lorry drivers.

'Are you fuckin' mad?'

I neither saw them, nor heard them. I wouldn't have noticed if one had run right over me. I was still wearing my jaunty navy-blue hat.

Beginning

I remember the next time I saw you, waiting, waiting for you to arrive. I looked out of the window and there you were, hesitating a bit at the gate, taller than I had imagined, but the same face, the same face.

I waited for you to ring the bell before opening the door. I didn't want to rush you, to alarm you. I waited, hardly breathing. One more minute. Only one more minute of patience. Not hard after twenty-two years. Sister Frances always said to believe in the prayer, 'In much patience shall thy peace be.'

In the years between, I often had to remind myself of that. At first I found it almost impossible to bear. I wanted not to be. I dreamt nightly of your crying self and would wake looking for the cot, looking for you, truly believing you were in the next room. I had no desire to even wake up, let alone work. When I was asleep and dreaming, you were somehow closer.

Just after your first birthday I wrote to the adoption society, asking them if you were happy, if you were loved. I had a letter some time later saying that, although it was not strictly usual, an official had visited you and your family and that you were very happy and jolly, that you were learning to walk and that you were still called Louise. It also said that your mother was very sad for me and would pray for me. So I knew you were all right – you were well loved.

Around this time, Frank gave me a tough talking to. I was living in a slouching Slough of Despond, not working, not going out, scrounging off the family. He told me to move myself and do something. Anything. Scrub floors. Anything. But get moving. So, I did. Back to work, in a café, in a school, in a music hall. Slowly. Back to life.

It wasn't until 1969 that I finally fell in love with the man who renewed my hope, gave me purpose and unconditional love. John Alderton, the tall gangling actor I didn't quite say hello to in *Emergency Ward 10*. He always shared my belief that one day you would make contact, hoped for it as much as I did. Indeed over the years we often talked about when we should tell our children, Nic, Kate and Rich, that they had an older sister. We didn't want to raise their hopes in case you decided not to look for me.

In spring 1986, I found myself constantly wondering if you would try to find me, now that you were twenty-one. I started to shoot more complex thoughts into the ether, than my little daily arrow.

'I'm here if you want me.'

'You may not want me and that's OK. But I am here.'

One day Kate suddenly said the one thing missing from her life was a sister. She wished she had a sister.

In the middle of May I started to dream about you every night, vivid insistent dreams, mostly of you as a baby, but some of you as a little girl just standing beside me, smiling and laughing.

Then about a week later I opened an unremarkable brown envelope and there was your letter.

I was speechless with joy, but not surprised. I couldn't believe the wonder of it and yet I'd always known it would happen.

The most marvellous thing about that first letter was the sense I had of a strong and centred young woman. I learned that your mother had more children after you. That was a surprise. And that you were about to take your finals for a French degree. So you love French too!

But most of all as I read, I was overwhelmed by your

kindness and understanding towards me. You even gave me an out! You said that you wanted me to know you'd had a good life but that if I didn't wish to reply you quite understood. How little you knew me. I was then and still am astonished by your lack of resentment towards me. If you feel it, you are great-hearted enough never to show it. Although maybe in a few years, when we know each other better, you'll be able to say, 'Now, you old bat. I *am* angry with you!' Maybe!!

Over the next few weeks we exchanged long letters and phone calls and arranged to meet. I told the family the wonderful news. John, of course, was crying and delighted. Kate wept buckets and wrote you a long letter. Nic patted me on the head several times and said, 'Well done, Mum!' And Rich just grinned from ear to ear.

And then there we were, as I opened the door both smiling, hardly believing.

'Hello.'

'I'm Louise.'

'I know. It's lovely to see you.'

'I'm really pleased to see you.'

Inadequate, inane, ineffectual words. But it didn't matter.

And with unbelievable ease we slipped back into each other's lives.

In the dark days when guilt and anguish hit me like a punch in the stomach, I used to try to remember the image I had of the slim, fair woman who was your mother, and focus on the good things of your life. They were all true.

The first time I met Maria there she was, the woman I'd always pictured, welcoming me into her home. And can you remember my wonder when she brought out your yellow pram suit and the shawl I'd wrapped you in, twenty-two years later?

As we talked about that day, it was extraordinary to know at last what was happening on the other side of the door. How your dad was chastised for leaving their room to get your carrycot just about the time I was trying to leave the building. Sad too to find out that your little wicker suitcase never made it to your family. They received your clothes in a bin bag. Maybe the agency was afraid I'd sewn some terrible, embarrassing message in the lining. What they overlooked, however, was the fact that I'd forgotten to unpick my initials from the nappies. P.C. in yellow chainstitch. Maria told me.

Sitting in your home with your mum, I was aware of a tremendous sense of the familiar. It felt like my home, my family. I felt I'd known Maria all my life. Maybe it's the northern thing as she comes from Salford. Maybe it's Catholicism which makes us all curiously members of the same tribe.

Soon after I was able to put you in touch with Tony and his wife Janet. He's been living only a mile or so away from you all these years. I'd never completely lost contact with him and we'd worked together a couple of times. I didn't know he had a little girl, Aïlésa, and another one on the way. He met you at the beginning of July and Alana was born at the end. Two daughters in one month! Now they have Lily too.

Everyone was at your wedding, all the brothers and sisters and six parents! And now, around the time of your next birthday, you'll have a baby. And so the wheel turns.

I never cease to wonder at how lucky I am that you chose to find me. Nor to be grateful to Maria for her generosity of spirit. When we talk about you she calls you 'our daughter'.

I'll never forget either the first time I met your grandma. As we sat having a cup of tea she said very firmly, 'She won't leave her mother, you know.' And although we all laughed and I assured her I would never expect you to, it made me think about what place there is for me in your life. I think the only vacancy is maternal aunt! Maria never had a sister and talking together recently she's let me be an honorary one. So maybe that's for me. An aunt who hasn't seen you for a long, long time who doesn't really know you, but who loves you.

In the dark years, I used to write poems about how little I had given you in life. One began, 'Mother, you gave me nothing,' and ended, 'Daughter, I gave you away.'

But I didn't give you nothing. I gave you your dear dad and your handsome loyal brothers. I gave you Bern, the sweetest, most loving sister imaginable.

And I gave you the best mother in the world. I gave you Maria – your mother.

I couldn't possibly have given you better.

All my love,
Pauline

LONDON, NEW YEAR'S DAY, 1992

NOT WITHOUT MY DAUGHTER
by Betty Mahmoody

'You are here for the rest of your life. Do you understand? You are not leaving Iran. You are here until you die.'

Betty Mahmoody and her husband, Dr Sayyed Bozorg Mahmoody ('Moody'), came to Iran from the USA to meet Moody's family. With them was their four-year-old daughter, Mahtob. Appalled by the squalor of their living conditions, horrified by what she saw of a country where women are merely chattels and Westerners are despised, Betty soon became desperate to return to the States. But Moody, and his often vicious family, had other plans. Mother and daughter became prisoners of an alien culture, hostages of an increasingly tyrannical and violent man.

Betty began to try to arrange an escape. Evading Moody's sinister spy network, she secretly met sympathisers opposed to Khomeini's savage regime. But every scheme that was suggested to her meant leaving Mahtob behind for ever . . .

Eventually, Betty was given the name of a man who would plan their perilous route out of Iran, a journey that few women or children had ever made. Their nightmare attempt to return home began in a bewildering snow-storm . . .

'The horrific situation in which Betty Mahmoody found herself would give any loving mother nightmares. Hers is an amazing story of a woman's courage and total devotion to her child that will have you rooting for them along every inch of their treacherous journey'
Susan Oudot, *Woman's Own*

0 552 13356 6

THE ROAD AHEAD
by Christabel Bielenberg

Following the extraordinary success of her wartime memoirs, *The Past is Myself*, Christabel Bielenberg received thousands of letters from readers begging her to describe what happened next. *The Road Ahead* takes up the story at the moment the first volume left off – with the outbreak of peace.

Germany was devastated by war and its aftermath, while Britain seemed grey and exhausted. Christabel joined the rebuilding of a defeated nation but Peter's near-fatal accident and her own illness made the young couple decide to turn their backs on England and Germany and make a new start farming in Ireland. Life was harsh at first, but predictably Christabel found humour in the many mishaps of country life while the beautiful scenery of the Wicklow Mountains provided a haven for all who visited them.

Her readers will be enchanted by this second volume of memoirs, as clear-sighted and generous, as honest, funny, touching and brave as *The Past is Myself*.

'Christabel Bielenberg writes like a dream'
Peter Mullen, *Daily Mail*

0 552 99469 3

MARTHA JANE & ME
A Girlhood in Wales
by Mavis Nicholson

Today Mavis Nicholson rubs shoulders with the famous. As a girl in South Wales in the thirties and forties, she dreaded her friends finding out how closely she rubbed shoulders with Martha Jane, the grandmother whose large feather bed she had to share until she left home.

Mavis's funny and delightfully different childhood memoir conjures up her vanished world at 5 Mansel Street, Briton Ferry, the small terraced house crammed with grandparents, parents, brother and sister. She describes with humour and affection the daily round of work and play – the street games, the outings with the flamboyant Martha Jane, the weekly visits to the Kinema and Jerusalem Chapel, her grandfather's drunken exploits, her father's steelworks job, and her mother's gentle influence over the whole family. Above all, she recalls the bittersweet memories of her possessive, increasingly jealous grandmother, Martha Jane, the dominant influence in her young life.

Martha Jane & Me is a classic of its kind, an enchanting account of the joys and agonies of childhood, and an unforgettable evocation of a community, its characters and a way of life just half a century ago, but more than a world away.

0 552 99509 6

A SELECTION OF FINE AUTOBIOGRAPHIES AND BIOGRAPHIES
AVAILABLE FROM CORGI AND BLACK SWAN

THE PRICES SHOWN BELOW WERE CORRECT AT THE TIME OF GOING TO PRESS. HOWEVER TRANSWORLD PUBLISHERS RESERVE THE RIGHT TO SHOW NEW RETAIL PRICES ON COVERS WHICH MAY DIFFER FROM THOSE PREVIOUSLY ADVERTISED IN THE TEXT OR ELSEWHERE.

☐ 99065 5	THE PAST IS MYSELF	*Christabel Bielenberg*	£5.99
☐ 99469 3	THE ROAD AHEAD	*Christabel Bielenberg*	£5.99
☐ 99422 7	DAPHNE: A PORTRAIT OF DAPHNE DU MAURIER	*Judith Cook*	£5.99
☐ 13126 1	CATHERINE COOKSON COUNTRY	*Catherine Cookson*	£9.99
☐ 13407 4	LET ME MAKE MYSELF PLAIN	*Catherine Cookson*	£3.99
☐ 13928 9	DAUGHTER OF PERSIA	*Sattareh Farman-Farmaian*	£5.99
☐ 13669 7	DANGEROUS CANDY	*Raffaella Fletcher*	£2.99
☐ 99479 0	PERFUME FROM PROVENCE	*Lady Fortescue*	£5.99
☐ 99557 6	SUNSET HOUSE	*Lady Fortescue*	£5.99
☐ 99558 4	THERE'S ROSEMARY, THERE'S RUE	*Lady Fortescue*	£5.99
☐ 99418 9	A HOME BY THE HOOGHLY	*Eugenie Fraser*	£4.99
☐ 12833 3	THE HOUSE BY THE DVINA	*Eugenie Fraser*	£5.99
☐ 99425 1	A HOUSE WITH FOUR ROOMS	*Rumer Godden*	£5.99
☐ 99347 6	A TIME TO DANCE, NO TIME TO WEEP	*Rumer Godden*	£4.99
☐ 13944 0	DIANA'S STORY	*Deric Longden*	£3.99
☐ 13943 2	LOST FOR WORDS	*Deric Longden*	£3.99
☐ 13822 3	THE CAT WHO CAME IN FROM THE COLD	*Deric Longden*	£3.99
☐ 13356 6	NOT WITHOUT MY DAUGHTER	*Betty Mahmoody*	£4.99
☐ 99463 4	DOROTHY: MEMOIRS OF A NURSE	*Dorothy Moriarty*	£4.99
☐ 99509 6	MARTHA JANE AND ME	*Mavis Nicholson*	£5.99
☐ 13946 7	NICOLA	*Nicola Owen*	£4.99
☐ 13732 4	HOVEL IN THE HILLS	*Elizabeth West*	£3.99
☐ 13739 1	RED ROWANS AND WILD HONEY	*Betsy White*	£3.99
☐ 99512 6	NOBODY NOWHERE	*Donna Williams*	£5.99

All Corgi/Bantam Books are available at your bookshop or newsagent, or can be ordered from the following address:

Corgi/Bantam Books,
Cash Sales Department,
P.O. Box 11, Falmouth, Cornwall TR10 9EN

UK and B.F.P.O. customers please send a cheque or postal order (no currency) and allow £1.00 for postage and packing for the first book plus 50p for the second book and 30p for each additional book to a maximum charge of £3.00 (7 books plus).

Overseas customers, including Eire, please allow £2.00 for postage and packing for the first book plus £1.00 for the second book and 50p for each subsequent title ordered.

NAME (Block Letters) ....

ADDRESS ....

....